VARIETIES O
EXP

WIDER

Studies in Development Economics embody the output of the research programmes of the World Institute for Development Economics Research (WIDER), which was established by the United Nations University as its first research and training centre in 1984 and started work in Helsinki in 1985. The principal purpose of the Institute is to help identify and meet the need for policy-oriented socio-economic research on pressing global and development problems, as well as common domestic problems and their inter-relationships.

Varieties of
Stabilization Experience

Towards Sensible Macroeconomics
in the Third World

LANCE TAYLOR

CLARENDON PRESS · OXFORD

Oxford University Press, Walton Street, Oxford OX2 6DP

Oxford New York Toronto
Delhi Bombay Calcutta Madras Karachi
Petaling Jaya Singapore Hong Kong Tokyo
Nairobi Dar es Salaam Cape Town
Melbourne Auckland

and associated companies in
Berlin Ibadan

Oxford is a trade mark of Oxford University Press

Published in the United States
by Oxford University Press, New York

First published in hardback 1988
New as paperback first published 1991

British Library Cataloguing in Publication Data

Taylor, Lance
Varieties of stabilization experience:
towards sensible macroeconomics in the
Third World.
1. Developing countries. Economic
conditions. Stabilisation
I. Title
339.5'09172'4
ISBN 0-19-828638-4
ISBN 0-19-828731-3 (Pbk)

Library of Congress Cataloging in Publication Data
Data available

Printed and bound in Great Britain by
Biddles Ltd, Guildford and King's Lynn

PREFACE

For more than a decade now, most developing countries have been subject to a succession of shocks emanating largely from changes in the international economic environment. These shocks invariably disrupted the working of their economies, forcing on them relatively long periods of stabilization and adjustment to restore equilibrium conditions. How can developing countries cope with such situations? What are the policy options open to them? Until recently these questions were sought to be addressed largely within the framework of orthodox macroeconomics. This is reflected in the stabilization packages advocated by the International Monetary Fund for a large number of developing countries in the recent past. By and large these involved a set of austerity measures sweetened with conditional balance of payments support under the auspices of the international financial institutions. The degree to which this standard approach was relevant or successful was the focus of a WIDER research project involving a series of country studies. More specifically, the research focused on whether alternative policy packages could have been devised in particular country situations which would contribute to desirable adjustment and development goals, i.e., an improved balance of payments and higher growth rates, at a *lower* social cost than that incurred by the country packages that were in fact negotiated.

The general finding of the WIDER research studies was that countries were hard hit by the shocks; but adjusted in different ways, depending on their own local institutions, macroeconomic structure, and relationships among major political and social groups. The wealth of country-based experience has clearly established the need for a departure from the earlier perspective of a standard approach to the design of stabilization and adjustment programmes. The new ideas emerging out of the country studies highlight the need to formulate these programmes in a manner appropriate to the institutional and structural characteristics of the eocnomy in question.

Orthodox macroeconomics, as reflected in the approach of the International Monetary Fund to stabilization problems, ran mainly

in terms of attaining equilibrium within a narrow monetary
framework. In fact, this was defined as financial programming
towards the goal of stabilization. The WIDER country studies
provide ample evidence to suggest that there is no unified theory or
policy to facilitate solutions to problems of stabilization and
adjustment. A variety of policies involving a combination of
different approaches seems to have worked well, depending on the
peculiarities of country situations. What comes out clearly from the
WIDER country studies is the need to deal with each country
situation within the framework of its own specific economic and
social characteristics.

A unique feature of the WIDER stabilization studies is the fact
that most of the country authors are nationals, who have brought a
wealth of local knowledge and experience to an area of macroeconomics where the international discussion has for the most part been
dominated by economists proposing policy on the basis of ideas
popular in the developed world. The WIDER research findings in
this area have clearly established that current policy and practice
cannot be regarded as sacrosanct and needs to be modified if they
are to be relevant and effective in dealing with stabilization
problems in developing countries. In this context one should
welcome the widening debate on these issues and some of the recent
changes in policies advocated by the International Monetary Fund
in its recommendations for developing countries in Africa. WIDER
research will, I would hope, contribute to the evolving process of
identifying improved solutions to stabilization and adjustment
issues, without damaging the development process itself.

Lal Jayawardena
Director WIDER

ACKNOWLEDGEMENTS

If an academic author lifts ideas from two or three others, anyone would call it plagiarism. If she or he has access to ideas from 18 papers, then formulating a synthesis can safely be called 'research'. This monograph reports on the results of such research. The unsung contributions are papers describing experiences with economic stabilization in 18 developing countries, supported by the World Institute for Development Economics Research (WIDER) in Helsinki.

I am extremely grateful to WIDER, its staff, and its director, Lal Jayawardena, for sponsoring the stabilization project, and to Gerry Helleiner who did at least as much as I did to get it organized. Ford Foundation, personified by Tom Bayard, was also generous with research funding.

In writing up the project, I have benefited from comments and discussion by all its participants. Reg Green and Gerry Helleiner contributed pages and pages of written observations. John Toye chipped in with very astute remarks on a summary version of the results presented as the Marshall Lectures at the University of Cambridge in May 1987. Other comments came from Jose Pablo Arellano, Korkut Boratav, Jose Maria Fanelli, Roberto Frenkel, Bill Gibson, Butch Montes, Jose Antonio Ocampo, Michael Roemer, Jaime Ros, Pronob Sen, Andres Solimano, Rolph van der Hoeven, Richard Webb, and Tito Winograd. I have tried to do justice to them all.

Finally, my wife, kids, and pets put up with the burdens of authorship with their usual grace. Mick, in particular, deserves a vote of thanks for spending many hours wedged between the globe, bookshelf, and PC, trying to figure out what was going on. He probably succeeded as well as did the author.

WIDER Stabilization and Adjustment Policies and Programmes Country Studies

CONTENTS

1

Economic Stabilization in the Third World

Early this century, William James published the thoughts on religion which suggested this essay's theme. James was concerned to show that diverse religious experiences all probe a common well of subconscious spiritual strength. When one considers economic stabilization in developing countries, an obverse generalization applies. Stabilization packages share many elements in common, thanks to the tenets of orthodox economics and the ministrations of the World Bank and International Monetary Fund which preside over the ceremonies in most cases. But they give the most diverse results. The task at hand is to explain why, and offer suggestions on the basis of experiences with stabilization about how it can be done better.

Economies have to be stabilized when they are shocked. Macroeconomic shocks in avalanche proportion hit developing countries from the mid-1970s. From abroad, adverse movements in the terms of trade, the debt and interest-rate crises at the turn of the decade, and (in some cases) foreign exchange bonanzas destroyed external balance. Internal dislocations—hyperinflations, financial collapses, irresponsible policy teams, and natural disasters—added to the onslaught. Unusually for economic cycles, the magnitude of these events has not diminished over ten years.

Attempts at stabilization began worldwide, riveting policy to the short run. Both the shocks themselves and the responses were large—current account deficits exceeding ten per cent of GDP and inflations measured in double digits per month led to packages creating labour unemployment rates exceeding twenty per cent, output losses of more than ten per cent, and complete restructurings of local financial systems. Many countries are just emerging from these episodes. It is high time to ask what factors made the stabilizations work out as they did, and what mare's nests they leave for the future.

Most stabilizations in developing countries are not carried out by local authorities alone. For reasons discussed in Chapter 2 (mostly having to do with access to external resources), they work with international agencies. The two most commonly involved are the Bretton Woods institutions—the World Bank and especially the International Monetary Fund. The Fund's pre-eminence in stabilization reflects the division of labour set up for the institutions when they were founded at the end of World War II. However, when ostensibly short-term problems extend over the years, the borders of the Bank's long-term growth jurisdiction begin to be crossed. And at the same time, secular improvements in economic performance presumably require actions here and now. Hence, both agencies often have a hand in stabilization exercises, though they are usually better described as Fund/Bank rather than Bank/Fund affairs.

Typical IMF 'stand-by' arrangements with a country are described in Chapter 5. They amount to a line of credit tied to a macroeconomic programme set out in a Letter of Intent negotiated between local authorities and the staff of the Fund. The credits and policy guidelines go together under the name of 'conditionality' and the country can draw upon the Fund's loan if it satisfies 'performance criteria' specified in the Letter of Intent. Occasionally, the Bank is the contact agency for a programme with the Fund monitoring its execution, but such formal variations do not affect short-run conditionality's content. Longer term programmes of the form now becoming more common in sub-Saharan Africa enhance the Bank's role, as discussed in Chapter 5.[1]

Programmes undertaken by the Bretton Woods agencies resemble one another. To the first approximation, they are based upon the 'orthodox' approach to macroeconomics in the Third World. As we will see in Chapter 4's stabilization vignettes, specific packages may embody unorthodox elements. Some Fund/Bank staff members (practitioners more often than theoreticians) are open to unconventional actions and thoughts. However, the central tendency of the

---

[1] Even after one-year stand-by arrangements are negotiated, the Bank may soon add its own longer-term policy conditions to the Fund's performance criteria; commercial banks and donor agencies jump into the conditionality game as well. Avramovic (1986) describes the problems for local policy-makers that all these restrictions entail.

agencies' approach to short-term policy is clear, and clearly reflected in practice. Since orthodox remedies are widely applied, it makes sense to take a good look at how they work. Their weaknesses and strengths are analyzed here at length; other approaches (some tried in practice) are proposed to increase stabilization's benefits and reduce its costs. To trace orthodoxy's implications through, one must combine economic theory with lessons from experience, while trying to invent alternative policies as useful as possible for practical ends. A few words are in order about the empirical and analytical foundations of the ideas in this essay.

Country-level information comes mostly from 18 studies of recent stabilizations that were commissioned by the World Institute for Development Economics Research (WIDER), a branch of the United Nations University with its seat in Helsinki. The studies were co-ordinated by Gerry Helleiner and Lance Taylor, and are available from WIDER and will be published in due course. The countries covered are Mexico, Nicaragua, Colombia, Peru, Chile, Argentina, and Brazil in Latin America; Egypt, Sudan, Kenya, Tanzania, Ghana, and the Ivory Coast in Africa; and Turkey, India, Sri Lanka, the Philippines, and South Korea in Asia. All underwent one or more stabilizations over the past decade or so, and the studies provide a rich source of comparative evidence and analysis.

The papers are sensible and realistic: most were written by nationals and the rest by expatriates with substantial first-hand experience in the countries concerned. The authors' interpretations of events are eclectic; they provide independent bases for assessing how well mainstream approaches worked out. Their principal finding is that past policies could have been designed to better effect, and that programmes of the Fund/Bank type are optimal for neither stabilization nor growth and income redistribution in the Third World.

The WIDER authors arrive at these conclusions from theoretical stances different from the Bank's and Fund's. To varying degrees, they use 'structuralist' macroeconomic theory whereas most staff members of the agencies rely upon the 'neoclassical' and/or 'monetarist' formulations that have dominated North Atlantic economic thought for the past thirty years. As discussed in Chapter 3, the two approaches have been visible in economics for a long time, interacting over three centuries of the history of thought. Toye (1987) observes that in Latin America we are now witnessing 'Round Two' of the most recent monetarist/structuralist clash over inflation. Both sides learned something from Round One in the 1960s—monetarists that stabilization has to be validated by long-term institutional changes, and structuralists that inflation has causes besides supply rigidities and social conflict. The views of the authors reflect this and earlier debates: they draw on the insights of both camps.

One should not make too much of doctrinal niceties when decisions that affect hundreds of millions of people are at stake. However, the theoretical presumptions of economists *do* mould their policy suggestions. Someone who profoundly believes that either 'printing too much money' or 'irreconcilable social conflict' is the unique cause of inflation is unlikely to have his or her mind changed by arguments or evidence to the contrary. Arguments can always be rebutted. In macroeconomics especially, epicycles can be added to models to explain away inconvenient facts. For these reasons it pays to be clear about the intellectual baggage behind any particular stabilization scheme. Much of the discussion here is devoted to spelling out the reasoning supporting different policy moves, and how their effects will depend on the historical and institutional conditions of the economy at hand. This is the essence of a reasonable approach to stabilization and other economic problems.

The argument is separated into four chapters. Chapter 2 takes up the background for policies—the nature of internal and external shocks, and political constraints. This last topic leads into a discussion of the 'social matrix' within which stabilizations must unfold.

Chapter 3 is devoted to macroeconomic dynamics and structure—the means by which overall demand–supply balance is attained, price–cost relationships, factors affecting the balance of payments and financial markets, and other market considerations (black and grey). What seems an obvious point—that in thinking of a national economy one must always bear in mind its institutional relationships and the major lines of causality in its economic system—is emphasized in Chapter 3. In the jargon, plausible models of different economies will have different rules for the determination of equilibrium, or 'closures'. The chapter concludes with a checklist of guidelines for selecting a model structure appropriate to the economy at hand.

Chapter 4 summarizes the experiences of the 18 WIDER countries, dividing them into five categories based on the analysis of Chapter 3: economies subject to foreign exchange dearths or bonanzas, those in which income distributions and/or 'heterodox shocks' against inflation played an essential role in recent stabilizations, and India and South Korea as somewhat special cases. Approaches to stabilization appropriate to each category are discussed.

Chapter 5 begins with 15 thesis–antithesis pairs that summarize the results in Chapters 2 to 4; on the whole, the Bretton Woods approach comes down on the market-oriented side of the contrasts. Next comes a presentation of the usual IMF methodology for stabilization (called 'financial programming'), followed by constructive suggestions about how this standard operating procedure can be modified to deal with important macroeconomic linkages beyond its capability to address. Other perspectives on stabilization are briefly summarized, and the chapter closes with considerations about how stabilization can be extended toward growth and progressive income distribution in the medium run.

2

Macroeconomic Shocks and the Social Matrix

There are at least five goals that the policy teams trying to steer all economies share:

1. To maintain socially acceptable levels of capacity utilization and growth, especially in sectors and regions dominated by their political base;
2. To keep inflation down to a rate tolerable in terms of the country's own history of price increases and social defences against them—a 'tolerable' rate might range from something pretty close to zero in India to 100 per cent per year in South America's Southern Cone;
3. To alter national wealth and income distributions in line with their regime's own ideological predilections and political constraints;
4. To maintain some degree of self-reliance in trade and external financial relationships, in several dimensions to be elaborated as we proceed;
5. To strive for the first four goals in an environment free from undue economic shocks.

When shocks are so strong that the policy focus shifts almost completely towards off-setting them, the economy may be said to be going through a stabilization episode. Countries in the Third World have been in such a situation for most of the past decade.

Shocks can come from external events, internal mishaps, or both. Descriptions of disturbances so severe that they have to be stabilized are presented below. Externally, they include worsening of the foreign trade position (typically due to adverse world price shifts or falling export volume), improvements in the trade position (a foreign bonanza), unfavourable shifts in service trade (interest obligations up or foreign remittances down), and movements in the capital account (inflows decline or are cut off). Problems originating internally include capital flight on the part of national asset-holders, a local financial crisis, unacceptably rapid inflation, and attempts to change the medium-term policy course. In some cases stabilization has been required to counter the errors of previous regimes: excessively expansionary policy, reckless exchange rate management, and precipitate trade or exchange liberalization were the most common mistakes. Finally, many countries in the Third World have recently been hit by natural or man-made disasters (harvest failures, wars) which disrupt the economy from the side of supply.

As already noted, when developing countries undertake stabilization they do so in collaboration with the International Monetary Fund and/or the World Bank. There are inducements and pressures toward this course. Both institutions tie disbursement of their own lines of credit to an acceptable programme. They are generally thought to provide a 'seal of approval' which eases access to private capital markets as well as official support in the form of increased foreign aid, Paris Club debt reschedulings, and so on. The WIDER studies show that the proffered foreign exchange does not always arrive, but its promise still acts as a strong incentive. So does political and economic pressure which industrialized countries may exert on the Fund's potential clientele.

Governments may agree to Fund/Bank terms readily, or there may be extended conflict and disagreement—the country studies include examples of both sorts. Even without the presence of external agents and their conditionalities, however, there are common elements reappearing in stabilization attempts in rich and poor countries for the past 150 years. They typically include five sorts of policy changes:

1. 'Austerity' in the sense that the public sector is expected to contract its fiscal deficit (in real and even nominal terms), and borrow less from the central bank. The means chosen typically include cuts in state spending for public investment and social service programmes, plus higher prices for products supplied by public enterprises and increased taxes.

2. Revision of the exchange rate, in most cases directed towards weakening or devaluation. Appreciation is occasionally recommended on anti-inflation grounds.

3. Monetary tightness, involving not only restrictions on credit to the public sector, but also reduced private credit limits, interest rate increases, and similar manoeuvres as applicable in the institutional context.

4. Policies aimed at improving economic performance in the medium term. Since the Fund and Bank are market-oriented, their suggestions usually include 'liberalizing' the system by removing state interventions in domestic markets, lowering trade barriers, and easing off on exchange controls. More specific recommendations may include interest-rate increases (consistent with tight money) aimed at raising saving, cuts in the real wage, price incentives for exporters and/or food producers, etc. Usually though not always, non-price supply policies such as directed planning and public investment are given short shift.

5. Income policies consistent with the manoeuvres just enumerated are used to redirect specific payments flow—wage restraint, revision of subsidy and transfer programmes, and stimuli for import substitution or export promotion which favour certain economic groups are frequently observed.

For most economies in the WIDER studies, IMF packages included fiscal austerity, monetary tightness, currency devaluation, liberalization in various forms, and wage restraint. Other policy moves were added in specific contexts. As already noted, at times additional international finance was released by a Letter of Intent with the Fund, and at times not. But regardless of capital inflow, tracing through the direct effects of orthodox stabilization is a matter of enormous practical concern. How policies might be modified to make stabilization less painful is another major issue. We take up both queries after reviewing the nature of shocks and their effects in more details.

2.1 Internal Shocks

Accelerating inflation is the prime internal trigger for stabilization efforts. It also provides a touchstone to distinguish structuralist and orthodox/monetarist perceptions of macroeconomic shocks.

'Over-expansion' and 'excess demand' are potent words for mainstream economists, and often the general public as well. Monetarist stabilization is supposed to counter the inflationary pressures that result from such forces. However, the economics profession has never been unanimous in believing that the fundamental cause of inflation is emitting too much money. As Kindleberger (1985) observes, monetarists and structuralists with opposing views on the matter trace lineages of at least 300 years. In the monetarist camp appear the Cap party of small merchants in Sweden late in the seventeenth century, the British Currency School stemming from the work of Ricardo and Thornton, the American Chicago School, and most staff members of the International Monetary Fund. Structuralists include the big-merchant Hat party that opposed the Caps, the British Banking School, Keynesian economists generally, and the majority of the country authors for the WIDER project.

Monetarist inflation theory is a demand and supply fable. It says that the supply of money is determined independently of the rest of the system, largely by government borrowing from the central bank. Demand for money depends mainly on the price level, as well as the interest rate, pace of economic activity, etc. In the simplest monetarist story, these extra explanatory variables are set aside. Equating demand to supply of money implies that changes in the latter uniquely cause the price index to move— it is the only variable left free to adjust when the money supply varies. In the commodity-producing part of the economy, new monetary emission is supposed to signal excess demand for commodities, so that prices rise more or less proportionately to the growth of money supply. On the financial side, creating money raises 'real balances' (money supply divided by the overall price index) above the level desired by wealth-holders. They try to spend more, and the excess balances are liquidated by increasing prices.

The level of output is typically assumed constant (or determined solely from the supply side) in monetarist models. This hypothesis and the demand–supply story just narrated are formalized in an accounting relationship called the 'equation of exchange'. It states that money supply × velocity = price level × output. From this relationship it is easy to see that with output fixed, more money must drive the price level up.[1] Sophisticated versions of the same story are based on the notion of an 'inflation tax', and there are balance of payments implications as well. These extensions are taken up in Chapter 3.

Structuralist theory asserts that inflations result from two factors. The first is distributional conflict, often signalled by relative price shifts. The second is a set of rules for price formation that expands the conflict into a cascade of price increases throughout the system—a propagation mechanism. Both factors are woven tightly into the institutional fabric of the economy at hand, as are its members' tolerances for inflation.[2]

Conflicting distributional claims take several forms. Some social groups, for example workers under contracts with fixed money wages, may be hurt by price increases resulting from shortages of products subject to output (or import) limits. 'Excess' demands do trigger inflations in such cases, though only in connection with propagation mechanisms passing effects to other prices. Cascading wages and agricultural product prices are a familiar case, as in Brazil in 1986–87. Indeed, restricted agricultural supply as the prime cause of inflation has long been emphasized in the writings of the Latin American branch of the structuralists (for example, Noyola Vasquez 1956). For the German hyperinflation of the 1920s, Franco (1986) restates the structuralist line (espoused by conservative politicians at the time) that the conflict was between workers' aspirations for a high real wage, and the low wage implicit in an exchange rate weak enough to generate the trade surplus required to pay World War I reparations. Elsewhere, jumps in non-traded goods prices created by attempts to spend the proceeds of a foreign exchange bonanza within a country have sparked inflationary conflict. Mexico is a recent example.

Once their real income levels are hit by such prices changes, organized groups try to protect themselves against general inflation

[1] 'Velocity' or the ratio of the value of output to the money supply is treated as an institutionally determined constant in most IMF exercises. Empirically, its purported stability may be a bit shaky—one WIDER author (Reginald Green) calls it 'a triumph of will over data'. Alternatively, velocity may be assumed to rise when inflation is faster, as the public learns to use less money when its value is being eroded more rapidly by faster price increases.

[2] Canavese (1982) sets out several illustrative models.

by raising 'their own' prices: for example, workers strive for increased nominal wages. The stage is set for a price spiral as 'indexation' of price increases one to another appears. If indexation becomes firmly enough established, the initial conflict may vanish from notice as inflation turns 'inertial' with this period's average price increase becoming an unbiased predictor (perhaps with high variance) of the rise in each of next period's micro prices.

Structural inflation theory combines uneasily with the equation of exchange. Structuralists are more willing than monetarists to let output vary in their models: as we will see below, they delight in its determination through distributional and income effects. However, they still treat the level of activity as a variable determined by its own devices. To satisfy the equation of exchange, which is 'true' in a tautological sense, they ultimately have to let either the supply of money or velocity be endogenous. If monetary and fiscal policy are 'passive', a public sector deficit and/or loose credit restraints in effect ratify a continuous inflation by permitting the money supply to increase apace. Within some range, velocity as usually measured may rise as substitute means of payments (overdrafts, inter-firm debt, foreign exchange) are used in place of the local money. Through one channel or another, the equation retains its validity *ex post*.

Of course, the casual status of money can always be changed by policy—tough enough austerity makes it pre-determined instead of endogenous. One test of structuralist theory is to ask whether attempts to slow inflation purely by tight money will be effective. The WIDER studies show that such policies seem more often than not to fail.[3] On the other side of the coin, 'heterodox shock' anti-inflationary packages directed solely at removing indexation by state fiat fail if they ignore the first component of structural price increases, i.e. underlying distributional conflict.

A considered judgement is that one or other of the two theories applies better, depending on circumstances. As discussed below, a predominance of price-clearing markets and absence of indexation provide an institutional environment congenial to monetarism. However, even under highly structuralist conditions as in Argentina recently, non-expansionary policy may make heterodox shocks

---

[3] A compilation of the successes and failures of attempts to reduce inflation by monetary restraint in the WIDER sample of countries appears in Chapter 4.

more likely to succeed. In any specific context, some blend of the two approaches makes sense, since neither theory can claim to be decisively correct.

Two final points should be noted. First, public opinion may be monetarist, for diverse reasons. The theory is easy to package and sell, appeals to critics of an interfering government, and may be massively propagandized by communications media representing the financial point of view. As a consequence, structuralist stabilizations such as the one in Argentina in 1985–86 may have to be camouflaged as 'austere'.[4]

Second, inflation rates that create calls for stabilization vary widely across countries, and depend on their class structures. Habitual debtors like farmers and small businessmen favour inflation; habitual creditors like bankers and rentier elements do not. At times, net asset positions appear in surprising places: for example, African export farmers are net creditors of the crop marketing boards, and dislike inflation because it threatens the boards' always precarious financial health. Elsewhere, South Korean middle classes opposed inflation more in the 1970s than in the decade before when they gained from super-growth. In India, the bourgeoisie has always been stoutly anti-inflationist while most policy-makers assert that shielding the poor from price increases is a major part of their task—deeply-held beliefs (and social positions) are obviously at stake. What is perceived as a 'moderate' rate of price increase depends on the economy's own history of inflation and the degree of indexation of its contracts and returns on assets. The WIDER studies provide a wide range of evidence on this topic.

Besides inflation, other internal events require stabilization. One is financial chaos. In several country examples, a financial crisis followed over-enthusiastic liberalization of banking regulations and relaxation of exchange controls. Prudent state intervention has long been recognized as essential to stabilize financial

---

[4] One should note that the public can learn to be anti-monetarist as well. One of the authors of the WIDER paper on Chile (Andres Solimano) observes that in his country monetarist '. . . orthodoxy is identified with regressive income redistribution, permanent squeezes on real wages, debt indexation for medium and small size domestic debtors, etc. Most of these policies are indeed very unpopular.'

markets. When it is suddenly abolished, bubbles and Ponzi schemes abound.[5]

Three examples illustrate the pattern. In newly deregulated Turkey, small financiers jumped into niches opened in an oligopolistic banking structure. The 17-year old 'Banker Yalcin' set up an office on loans, almost equalled Ponzi in paying seven per cent monthly interest on deposits, took new deposits to pay the interest, and ran away to Syria before his scheme collapsed.

On a grander scale, Chilean groups with nicknames like Piranhas and Crocodiles used banks in their control to set up conglomerates of firms denationalized at knock-down prices by the government after the 1973 Pinochet *coup*. In a high interest rate and low investment economy, each group borrowed from its bank to bid up its own companies' shares in a stock market and real estate boom. The bubble expanded for a time, inflated by capital inflows and local saving which could not find an outlet in real capital formation. In the final reckoning the government had to renationalize many of the companies and refinance the banks when their bad loans could no longer be concealed. Those with political clout—including foreign lenders in the liberalized capital markets—received greatest protection in both Turkey and Chile.

Third, the whole Philippine economy effectively played a Ponzi game in 1983 after the Marcos regime had engaged in massive, foreign-financed investment projects that failed. The nation recurred to increasingly short-term, high-cost external debt to meet the interest on prior borrowing that did not pay off.

Countries with internal financial tangles often have added problems of capital flight. Argentina presented a classic case in the late 1970s. A strongly market-oriented policy team pre-announced a low rate of exchange depreciation, in an 'active' crawling peg policy aimed at reducing inflationary expectations and containing price increases directly through the 'law of one price' (described more fully in the next section). At the same time the government

[5] Charles or Carlo Ponzi operated in Boston in 1920. According to Kindleberger (1978) he promised to pay 50 per cent interest on 45-day deposits, to use in arbitrage operations between depreciated foreign currencies and International Postal Union coupons which could be exchanged for US stamps. He took in $7.9 million and held only $61 worth of stamps when he was arrested. His ingenuity in using newly borrowed money to pay his prior obligations did not exceed that of more recent operators in developing countries, as the text describes.

lifted capital controls. Inflation was structural and did not slow; the consequence was increasing overvaluation. As the current account deteriorated, fears of exchange depreciation spread, and wealth-holders put their assets abroad through the porous market. They were rewarded in the end by maxi-devaluation, but not before the government had run up enormous external debts to finance both the current account deficit and capital flight in the tens of billions of dollars. Two policy mistakes—wilful overvaluation and removing exchange controls—left completely avoidable debt and deflation problems for subsequent economic teams to try to clean up.

Two more internal causes of stabilization are political breakdown and unrealistic defence of the level of economic activity against external shocks by demand creation. Examples of the latter include Tanzania and Brazil. Tanzanian budgets underestimated the foreign exchange losses induced by falling terms of trade and the Idi Amin war for several years in the early 1980s; as a consequence the economy veered towards stagflation. Brazil followed a similar course after interest rate and oil price increases in the late 1970s. The errors—more visible with hindsight than beforehand—involved excessive optimism on the external front. Measures aimed at trade improvement could have been pursued sooner, although in both countries rational policy choice was not helped by the interminable conflict between local economists and teams sent by the Fund and Bank.

Ghana extended an initial failure of stabilization in the early and middle 1960s to national demoralization that lasted two decades. The military governments in the middle of the 1970s could be said not to have had operational economic policies at all. A recent reversal required the accession to power of a strong, reformist regime.

In Ghana, as elsewhere, politicians fell back on expansionist and distributive manoeuvres in trying to retain power. The story is common enough before elections in any democracy, but gets taken to extremes as persons in office sense that the old order is starting to fail. Turkey and Sri Lanka in the 1970s provide examples, as weakened governments lost control of much of the economy, including the strings of the fiscal purse. In an inflationary twist, wage increases far greater than recent price rises were allowed in Argentina by a discredited military regime in 1983: they kicked off triple-digit annual inflation. Policy teams that inherit such econo-mies must deal with the predictable consequences—inflations truly set off by wage escalation or excess demands for non-tradables like food and/or goods with high import content, as well as yawning foreign exchange gaps. The Sandinista government in Nicaragua faces similar problems, amplified from abroad. Politics does impinge on economics, especially on the stabilization front.

Finally, natural or man-made disasters require stabilization, especially when they reduce availability of commodities (food, export crops) in chronically short supply. A disaster may be immediate, like an earthquake or an invasion, or stretch out over time. Droughts or excessive rains over months and years figure in recent economic history in many countries (especially in sub-Saharan Africa), causing inflation and output loss. Wars were important in the WIDER sample only in Tanzania, Nicaragua, and (to an extent) Argentina, but a glance at the map shows that they matter elsewhere in the world. It often takes time for the enormity of such events to sink in: the IMF as late as mid-1984 was blaming Peruvian economic chaos on excessive deficit spending when the 'El Nino' ocean current inversion that began in December 1982 had long since unleashed rains that flooded more than five per cent of GDP away. If investment is cut back as a consequence of such events, the internal shock can create echoes in the form of capacity shortages that persist for years.

2.2 External Shocks

External payments on any account—merchandise trade, net services, capital flows, or reserve changes—are not visible in the goals of growth, stable prices, and income distribution mentioned above. They just lurk behind the scene. The problem they create is that domestic targets are unattainable unless the balance of payments permits them to be met. How external factors can destabilize the economy is the topic of this section. As background, it is useful to begin with a description of the external conditions that most developing countries confront.[6]

Their imports are mostly made up of intermediate products and capital goods. Import substitution has been adopted worldwide as a

[6] For detail on external constraints in poor countries, see Taylor (1987a).

vehicle for development. It effectively replaces final commodity imports with domestic processing activity dependent on imported raw material and intermediate inputs. Hence, keeping local capacity in operation requires foreign exchange. There is a further twist on the side of investment. Import substitution rarely extends to machinery and equipment, yet these producers' goods comprise roughly half the value of gross fixed capital formation in all economies. Imported commodities thus become doubly scarce. Effective utilization of capacity depends on the intermediates; future growth requires investment with a high import content. When dollars are scarce, a poor economy faces a hard choice between sacrificing current output or maintaining and building up capital for growth.

On the side of exports, for reasons going far back into economic history, specialization in primary commodities is the rule in the Third World. Most developing countries began as economic and/or political colonies of central powers, and had primary product specialization forced upon them in the international division of labour of the nineteenth century. Even after decades of independence and pursuit of growth based on import substitution or export promotion, only a few economies (the newly industrializing countries, or NICs) have broken the historical mould. For the past ten years, world prices for primary goods have declined and in the mid-1980s were at a secular low. At the same time, export volumes stagnate because of the slow growth of industry worldwide. The consequence for the exporters is restricted capacity to import, especially painful in small nations open to trade. Many WIDER studies—for sub-Saharan Africa, Sri Lanka, Nicaragua, Peru, and Chile—emphasize this point.

Accounts on service and factor trade are in no better shape. For major debtor countries in the WIDER sample such as Argentina, Brazil, South Korea, and Mexico (and also for smaller economies whose debt/GDP ratios are equally great), high real interest rates since the late 1970s have multiplied current burdens for repayment; nominal rates have risen while the external terms of trade (the appropriate deflator) show negative growth. Poorer borrowers have been handicapped by the real decline in foreign aid inflows over the same period. Countries with emigrant labour forces have seen their real remittances drop.

Finally, these observations together suggest that trade in poor countries is 'non-competitive' in nature. Products imported are not produced at home, while major primary exports will have miniscule domestic markets. The implication is that many domestic products will not face direct competition from identical or similar foreign goods. Trade theory's 'law of one price' asserts that internal prices should tend towards world prices (times the exchange rate and taking into account trade barriers) in an open economy. But this equalization cannot occur if foreign and national goods do not freely compete. In terms of the workings of the law, most commodities in developing countries are effectively non-traded and subject to internal price-determination rules.

The external problem for most developing countries is restricted access to foreign exchange, for all the reasons just given. The lack of dollars leads to 'external strangulation', in a graphic phrase suggested by the United Nations Economic Commission for Latin America long ago. Strangulation forces output growth to lag and investment projects to be cut short because of unavailable imported inputs. Inflation may be kicked off as internal prices rise because of commodity shortages which cannot be offset by purchases from abroad. Import quotas and exchange controls may be stepped up, leading to the proliferation of grey or black markets and parallel transactions. Foreign resource constraints set the stage for stabilizations aimed at improving the balance of payments on all its constituent accounts.

Foreign exchange shortages are the most common cause of stabilizations in the Third World, especially in the recent period. However, gluts can create problems as well. They can arise from unexpected favourable shifts in export prices (coffee in Colombia and elsewhere) or new discoveries of exploitable resources (oil in Mexico in 1976). Without extreme counter-measures, part of a nation's increased foreign income will be channelled towards purchases of domestically produced goods, perhaps via increases in the money supply as rising central bank reserves prompt domestic credit creation. Prices of commodities which are in short supply and not easily tradable will rise. A structural inflation may be a consequence, as discussed above. A further problem is that with easy access to foreign exchange, policy-makers are in no hurry to devalue (itself an inflationary move) so that the exchange rate appreciates in real terms. Traditional export industries shut down, imports flood in, and the state itself may run an over-exhuberant monetary and fiscal policy—internal demand pressures are high while external diversification and self-reliance erode. With an appreciated currency, capital flight becomes appealing (and easy, if there are no exchange controls as in Mexico in the late 1970s). The flight may precipitate a payments crisis. The road is longer, but an initial excess supply of dollars can lead to many of the same problems as a shortage—especially if the bonanza peters out. Major debtors, recipients of the fruits of commodity booms like Colombia and Mexico, and beneficiaries of emigrant remittances and/or substantial foreign-aid flows like the Philippines and Egypt are all cases in point.[7]

As with inflation, economic doctrine provides no sure guide for dealing with external crises. Orthodoxy falls back on the powers of the price system to induce improvement by resource substitution. The postulated line of causality overlaps with the monetarist theory of inflation, and involves several steps. It begins with the premiss that austerity (reduced fiscal spending, tight credit, etc.) will lower aggregate demand. *If* output is fixed or determined from the supply side, then less demand should lead the overall price level to fall. However, one must distinguish between prices of non-traded and traded goods. *If* the law of one price applies, then traded goods prices will be determined from the world market; hence, austerity will lead only the prices of non-traded commodities to decline. Rising relative prices of tradables are the result. The shift should direct resources towards tradables, stimulating import substitution and export growth and improving the current account. Devaluation will help the process along, perhaps at some inflationary cost (it drives up prices of traded goods). Along with interest-rate increases, devaluation will also make holding domestic assets more attractive, reversing capital flight.

This story is self-consistent. Its problem is that it violates an

---

[7] Problems associated with foreign bonanzas are discussed sporadically by mainstream economists. There has been a recent upsurge in interest, under the rubric of the 'Dutch disease' (named after the consequences of major natural gas discoveries in the Netherlands). Corden (1984) gives a useful survey, without quite capturing the drama associated with such episodes in the Third World. Dutch disease problems are discussed further in Section 3.1.

ancient rule of thumb in applied economics: one should give minimal credence to arguments involving several steps, since each one of the linkages can easily be broken along the way. We have already observed that the law of one price is not enforced for most goods produced in a typical developing country; the assumption of fixed output also rarely applies. What usually happens under a demand-reduction programme is that the price mechanism is short-circuited. The cutback in real purchases makes production fall, cutting import needs directly. If, as all the WIDER studies emphasize, capital formation declines with austerity, then lower capital goods imports also help external balance. Exports of manufactures or primary products which are also wage-goods (for example, rice in Thailand or beef in Argentina) may go up as domestic absorption declines, but such responses are obviously country-specific. Primary product exports typically need more stimulus than just relative price shifts. Time and resource inputs such as investment programmes and/or marketing subsidies are required.

Price changes and demand contraction may not help non-commodity external balances either. Net service payments and capital flows have their own dynamics, dependent on expectations about growth and stability in the national economy which orthodox stabilization may not assure. Indeed, by holding down domestic investment, austerity may make repatriation of foreign incomes unattractive, as seems to be the case in Sudan.

The conclusion—argued more fully below—is that recovery from an external shock is a complex and painful process, irreducible to simple changes in relative prices. To understand the details, we will look at stabilization theory more fully in Chapter 3.

2.3 Political Considerations and the Social Matrix

Politics impinges on stabilization at all levels. The Bretton Woods agencies and external creditors themselves have a vivid political presence in developing countries. Their conditionalities may be diverted by local actors to their own ends. In one case (discussed in Chapter 4), the Marcos regime in the Philippines managed through financial ingenuity to transform IMF austerity into a vehicle for financing election campaigns. Elsewhere, Bretton Woods staff members have been at the focus of national debates on economic policy—Tanzania and Brazil are recent cases in point. Effectively, the agencies cannot avoid being caught up in politics: their technocratic teflon political coatings easily scratch away. Controversial policies they recommend—cutting food subsidies, major exchange-rate revisions, incomes policies which affect socially important groups—do not reduce their public exposure.

Strictly among citizens, we have already seen how political conflict can set off dynamic economic processes that ultimately need to be stabilized. Excessive expansion may be the last resort of a teetering regime; balance of payments problems or domestic inflation often result. Inflation can also be touched off by attempts at income redistribution that strain the social fabric. Once stabilization programmes are underway, their fate depends on the degree of political consensus or clout that the government can muster. Programmes meeting with some success in the WIDER sample—Turkey, Sri Lanka, Ghana, Argentina, Korea—occurred under regimes exercising effective repression or commanding substantial public support. Success in a stabilization exercise can of course add immensely to the prestige of a government, and aid it in other endeavours. The other side of the coin is that stabilization entails economic costs that must be borne by some or all social groups. This means that a government must draw (at times heavily) on its political resources to put a programme through. Unwillingness by politicians to act in the face of this fact means that stabilizations may be postponed or implemented inadequately, leaving worse economic problems for the future. Stabilization failures—in Ghana and the Philippines in the 1970s and the recent heterodox shock in Brazil among others—emphasize this point.

The WIDER studies approach these political issues via a 'social matrix' comprising political relevant groups, the major economic variables which affect them, and those variables over which they have some control. A few examples help illustrate the components of the matrix as identified in the country papers, and the economic roles they play.

The papers for Brazil, Egypt, India, and Sri Lanka suggest that concern for the economic position of 'the poor' may constrain policy decisions, though the poor themselves have no access to the levers of power. In Sri Lanka the deleterious effects of removing subsidies for rice consumption have been debated for years. The discussion helped prolong the life of the programme through the late 1970s. In Egypt the memory of food riots in January 1977 kept bread subsidies in force through to the time of this writing ten years later. The macroeconomic theory of Indian policy-makers as revealed in their pronouncements is monetarist; they restrain aggregate demand for fear of inflation. But they do so claiming that rising prices will undermine the fragile economic position of the poor through forced saving processes as discussed in Chapter 3. Finally, in Brazil at the turn of the 1980s a departing military regime restrained its economics ministers from policies that could worsen the country's already highly unequal income distribution. The generals apparently feared that distributional tension would make a backlash against participants in garrison rule more likely.

Certain groups of workers and/or agriculturalists may bear the brunt of stabilization efforts in specific countries and times. Recently in the Ivory Coast, non-Ivorian African workers lost jobs and suffered wage cuts induced by contractionary policy; in Sri Lanka workers on agricultural estates suffered from food price increases and the replacement of the rice subsidy by food stamps *not* indexed to inflation. Peasants and urban workers in Turkey were harmed respectively by reductions in crop support prices and incomplete wage indexation; rentiers and commercial capitalists benefited not only from these relative price changes but also from an export boom stemming from reduced domestic absorption of industrial products coupled with favourable foreign market conditions. There was a wage crunch in the 1960s but not the 1980s in Brazil, and in Mexico and Kenya recently but not a decade or two ago.

Profit recipients may also feel fluctuations in their income flows. Turkish export middlemen, for example, benefited from trade subsidies while peasant producers did not. In Kenya, both large plantation-owners and peasants producing tea and coffee gained income from similar programmes. Oligopolistic industrialists in Colombia may have been doubly harmed by contractionary stabilization as their mark-ups declined pro-cyclically; there appear to be counter-cyclical mark-up dynamics in Brazil.

Asset positions change in response to both valuations and returns. Devaluation was a widely-anticipated gift to those Argentines and Mexicans who engaged in capital flight. Debtors in dollars—the state and private firms—lost from the exchange-rate jump. High interest rates under monetarist stabilization imperil cash flows of firms dependent on bank finance for working capital needs: a wave of bankruptcies may follow. At the same time, changes in inflation rates impinge upon the asset positions of debtors and creditors in well-known ways. All these wealth effects may be sizeable under successful reductions of inflation. Their feedbacks into macro equilibrium are hard to foretell, and make economic management during the stabilization period a difficult art.

These examples suggest that different economic groups will be affected differentially by numerous factors: changes in relevant commodity prices, whether from market developments or state intervention; movements in the volume of output and its composition; asset revaluations and shifting rates of return. Each group wields stronger or weaker defences against adversity. Workers may or may not be able to achieve full indexation of their money wages or food-stamp allotments against inflation. Recently, Indian agriculturalists have been able to move the terms of trade in their favour by political influence over the regulatory process, and Tanzanians through parallel transactions as the government tried to force prices well below market-clearing levels. In other circumstances—Turkey and Sri Lanka—the state may hold considerable sway over the terms of trade. Inflation may force rentiers to accept negative real rates of return for at least a time. The balances of power always change, but strongly limit the actions a would-be stabilizer can take.

The moral is that getting into and out of economic stabilizations are not processes independent of major groups in the country, their political role, and insertion in the economic system. On the whole, professional economists deal uneasily with these issues, and often carry through their analyses of economic classes and their political roles ineptly. But such factors have been vital to the successes and failures of many stabilizations. The WIDER studies amply document this point, as we will see further in the descriptions of past stabilization attempts appearing in Chapter 4. In the future, one could also think of stabilizations 'with a human face', which would at least maintain the income and welfare positions of the poor and vulnerable groups in the society. This possibility, which can only be realized on the basis of a serious class analysis, is taken up in Chapter 5.

- Stagnation ✓
- ethlicration ✓
- models of closure

3

Stabilization Theory

Ideally, one ought to be able to teach macroeconomics at the university in the morning, advise the Minister on how to apply macroeconomics in the afternoon, and write scholarly papers on macroeconomics at night, all the while practising the same craft.[1] Such coherence does not characterize the work of most economists—lecture tropes, policy tricks, and (worst of all) theoretical prestidigitation do not blend easily in one mind. None the less, a macroeconomics for all seasons is a goal worth striving for. Its theoretical structure should be direct, easy to grasp, but still capable of dealing with all the complications that real economies present. Older macro-models embodied these precepts; more recent efforts conspicuously do not. In this chapter a rather old-fashioned theory based on stabilization experience in developing countries is set out, aimed at providing analysis of the past and prognosis for the future that students, ministers, and scholars can all use. In the interests of accessibility, the arguments are all in prose. Those with a taste for graphs and Greek letters can find the same material translated into algebra in Taylor (1983, 1987b).

The WIDER studies show that stabilizations are not all alike. They have different proximate and distant causes; unfold in diverse contexts of economic structure, institutions, and politics; and do not succeed to the same degree. Despite these contrasts, however, programmes do function in a macroeconomic environment that is broadly similar across market economies. Supplies and demands for nationally produced goods somehow come into equilibrium; the foreign balance of payments is also cleared. Prices decompose into components of cost; financial markets influence the rest of the economy, meanwhile adjusting themselves according to numerous

---

[1] A thought due to Roberto Frenkel, co-author of the paper on Argentina for the WIDER projects.

local rules. Aggregate supply–demand balance, price–cost relationships, external accounts, and financial markets intertwine in stabilization, in ways that differ across time and place. Lines of macroeconomic causality (or model 'closures') run differently in accordance with relevant aggregations of sectors, periods, and economic classes, not to mention a country's politics, institutions, and recent history.[2]

To sort out these linkages in this chapter, we first take up aggregate demand and supply conditions, perhaps the aspect of the economy most directly affected by the class differences summarized in each study's social matrix. We then discuss (in successive sections) price–cost relationships, balance of payments considerations, financial markets, and parallel transactions. Many macro 'effects' relevant to developing economies are pointed out along the way. They are summarized in the lengthy Table 1 which concludes the chapter in Section 3.6.

3.1 Demand–Supply Balance

The initial abstraction is a one-sector economy. Interactions between purely macro adjustment and income redistribution are often critical to the success of stabilization attempts, and are the first topic discussed. Generalizations to more sectors are considered next, and the section closes with a review of under-publicized macro linkages that the WIDER studies uncovered.

Most macroeconomic discourse revolves around the national income and product accounts. Parallel to the recognition in the accounts that economic activities both generate incomes and supply goods, macro models must include rules for the determination of

---

[2] The concept of 'closure' is slightly mystical, but is best illustrated by a difficulty that one encounters in school algebra. If there are more equations than variables in a problem, then usually one or more equations must be dropped to avoid an over-determined system. The reduced set of equations will be 'closed' mathematically, but the nature of its solution will obviously depend on which equations are left in or out. Sen (1963), Taylor (1983), Marglin (1985), and many others have observed that macroeconomic models tend to be over-determined in this sense—there are more 'reasonable' restrictions to be imposed on the system than there are variables to adjust. Debates about macro closure boil down to arguments about which equations might be dropped or what additional variables thrown in to give an algebraically consistent model. Mysticism enters by way of the beliefs about the nature of economics that different schools reveal through the equations and variables they select.

payments flows and the allocation of output. Aggregate supply in different specifications may be assumed fixed, somewhat elastic to price increases, or completely determined by demand. Supply conditions will be influenced by price and non-price policy interventions, as well as factors such as climate and the presence or absence of hostilities within a country or with its neighbours.

Output as augmented by imports which compete more or less directly with domestic products has several uses. It is distributed among intermediate sales, private and public consumption, investment (partly undertaken by the state), inventory changes, and exports. Production inputs include labour and intermediates, with a substantial proportion of the latter non-competitively imported in most developing economies. In a first approximation to be extended later, domestic income (essentially total value-added or GDP) is split into two primary flows—to wages and mark-ups or margins. The first question is how aggregate demand and supply are brought into equality. Two classic mechanisms (or model closures) show up worldwide—output variations and movements in the income distribution.[3]

Adjustment via output change follows a familiar path. If autonomous purchases or demand 'injections' (investment, exports, or government current spending) rise, economic activity immediately runs faster because of higher demand. More production means that income flows go up. After 'leakages' of imports and saving, the extra income generates consumer demand for national products. The added consumption cascades into a new, higher output equilibrium through the multiplier process. Austerity in the form of reduced state purchases or tight monetary policy reverses the sequence, forcing output to fall.

This mode of adjustment is well-known, and emphasized in the country studies. They also point out that an orthodox price-mediated shift from non-tradable to tradable goods production induced by austerity (see below and Section 2.2) does not occur. Nor need output be stimulated by wage-cutting—Keynes's *bête*

---

[3] The two adjustment modes trace a long way back in the literature. They are juxtaposed neatly in the work of Keynes. The *Treatise on Money* (1930) emphasizes distributional shifts. Five years later, the *General Theory* brought output adjustment to the eyes of the world. Amadeo (1986) maps the transition and contrasts Keynes's analysis with the 'stagnationist' approach of Michal Kalecki discussed below.

noire from the 1930s that keeps trying to creep into the Third World. The reasons why these orthodox policies do not often work are best understood in light of macro adjustment via shifts in distribution, the topic we take up next.

Distributional changes may permit macroeconomic equilibrium to be attained when output is fixed (or highly inelastic to changes in the price/cost ratio) in the short run. The upper bound on production could come from a shortage of capital or capacity in specific sectors (think of food as an example to be elaborated below), a foreign exchange constraint, or even full employment of labour. Price changes are central to the adjustment process, but they act not by inducing neoclassical substitutions of cheap commodities for dear but rather by modifying the income distribution to crowd out certain components of demand. The process works, *if* there are differing marginal propensities to save from different income flows in the system. In the discussion that follows, we follow convention in assuming that the saving rate from wage income is lower than that from mark-ups. In practice that is not the only differential at work. Saving propensities from government income, corporate earnings, the trade deficit, and other household receipts such as those of farmers are not equal, and real shifts in incomes flowing to all these groups play a role in the attainment of macro equilibrium.[4]

Suppose that demand injections rise, or supply contracts. One would naturally expect prices to go up. Under the production cost structure outlined above, higher prices must reflect into higher costs for labour and intermediate inputs, or higher mark-ups. If wages are not fully indexed to the price level, mark-ups will increase relative to wage payments and take up the slack. The income distribution shifts against labour, so the economy-wide share of saving in national income goes up. Household purchases decline to meet the autonomous spending jump, and excess commodity demand is inflated away.

Macro adjustment via 'forced saving' (or 'automatic lacking' in the English economist Dennis Robertson's phrase) due to higher exogenous demand or adverse supply shocks shows up in several

---

[4] Price changes also influence real wealth positions of different groups within the economy. They may modify their saving propensities as a consequence, giving rise to 'real balance' or 'inflation tax' responses which are discussed in Section 3.4. These wealth effects often (but not always) act in the same direction as the income-distribution changes discussed in the text.

country studies, where the movements in real purchasing power are mediated by changes in state-controlled as well as market-clearing prices. The cases of Turkey and Sri Lanka (with increased demand injections from exports and investment in irrigation works respectively) have already been mentioned. Forced saving can also kick off structural inflation, examples of which are given below.

In principle, austerity can make forced saving work in reverse. If a reduced demand injection does not directly force a decrease in output, it will be met by less rapidly rising mark-ups and a shift in the income distribution towards labour. In practice, such responses are more likely to follow an improvement in supply conditions, which may lead to slower inflation and progressive redistribution. In one important case, extra foreign exchange may release an import bottleneck, permitting domestic production to increase. To allow consumer spending to absorb the extra output, the overall saving propensity must decline. That is, margins must fall. A scenario along these lines helps explain part of the success of recent forex-intensive Bank/Fund programmes in sub-Saharan Africa (see the descriptions of experiences in Ghana and Tanzania in Chapter 4). A decade earlier, increased import capacity from an export boom in Tanzania in 1975–78 allowed cost-of-living inflation to fall from 50 per cent annually to the 10–15 per cent range within a few quarters.

The difference between the two adjustment mechanisms boils down to whether output or distribution responds to macroeconomic shocks. A little bit of both is what usually happens in practice, but it is useful to keep the distinction for analytical purposes. An obvious question when output adjusts is what will be the system-wide effects of exogenous distributional changes, taking into account feedbacks into demand. The answers help illustrate different perceptions of adjustment, and shed light on how the economy responds to 'income policies' such as wage-cutting.

The shock we consider is a *decrease* in the mark-up rate, arranged for example by social contract, wage indexation at rates exceeding 100 per cent of past inflation, price controls, or a liberal import policy. The income distribution would shift towards labour and stimulate consumption, pointing towards higher overall demand. However, as emphasized by Rowthorn (1982) and Dutt (1984) following an analytical tradition dating to Kalecki and before, the final outcome depends on additional factors.[5] For example, if a consumer-led expansion stimulates private capital formation in accelerator fashion, the economy may end up with higher capacity utilization (assuming that output is not already at capacity, employment, or foreign exchange limits) and faster growth. This scenario is traditionally called 'stagnationist', since redistribution activates an otherwise stagnant system. It can happen through channels besides the one just discussed, especially when more sectors than one are being considered (see below).

The other possibility is that reduced mark-ups or higher real wages make output fall, for example because of sticky investment and/or the drag on demand implicit in the higher relative price for imported intermediates that a lower mark-up entails. Higher profits or real wage cuts will then stimulate production in an 'exhilarationist' response. Orthodox policy proposals are often exhilarationist, although they down-play the significance of distributional change.[6] Their microeconomic foundation is substitution of labour for capital or intermediates when real wages decline. The substitution response leads to higher labour–output ratios, export expansion (because national products become cheaper in world markets), and more jobs. In the orthodox view, unemployment is 'classical' (in Keynes's use of the term) because labour costs too much.

The sign of the effect on output of changing real wages is a matter of practical interest. The WIDER country authors to a large extent view their economies as behaving in anti-classical, stagnationist fashion. In Kenya, Turkey, Brazil, Mexico, Argentina, Chile, and elsewhere lower wages or higher margins are said to make output fall from the side of demand. A partial offset (discussed in more detail below) may come from increased exports as domestic producers frustrated by weak local markets search for sales abroad. But typically, extra exports plus any substitution responses which may occur are not large enough to restore the overall level of

[5] Kalecki (1971) collects most of his papers on the topic at hand. Dutt and Rowthorn more directly follow Steindl (1951) in emphasizing accelerator effects in investment demand.

[6] The reason is that when output is fixed and neoclassical marginal productivity rules for demand for production inputs apply economy-wide, there is no room in a general equilibrium model for either exogenous distributional shifts or an independent demand injection creating forced saving. Kaldor (1955) emphasizes this aspect of over-determination—or closure—of the neoclassical system.

activity. Wage-cutting and other regressive policies often feature in orthodox stabilization packages. In a stagnationist economy they can lead to deep depression. Mexico, with its highly orthodox policies since 1982, provides a striking case. After four years of austerity and wage-cutting, an exhilarationist macroeconomic adjustment remains to be observed.

An obverse problem arises with progressive redistribution. If pushed too far, such a policy can drive demand up to output and/or inflation ceiling(s): as discussed in Section 2.3, the problem is most acute in politically weak, populist regimes. As an economy passes from the output to the forced saving adjustment mode, attempts at redistribution become self-defeating. Instead of making output rise, they can make the income distribution worse. The problem is the so-called 'paradox of thrift', which applies under forced saving. The usual somewhat fanciful illustration involves profit recipients who are assumed to provide the bulk of national saving. If one fine day they suddenly choose to consume a higher share of their income, then prices will rise to ration overall demand. With wages not fully indexed to the price increase, the income distribution will shift in the rentiers' favour to let them supply the saving required by a fixed level of demand injections. The paradox is that less thrift on the part of the profit recipients causes both their consumption and income to go up.

A more practical application involves the effects of attempts at income redistribution. When forced saving rules, the scenario for the poor runs against them. Attempts at distribution towards low savers will reduce the overall saving supply *ex ante*. *Ex post*, redistribution will be thwarted by contrary price shifts as savings requirements will be met. For example, unless supply is increased (perhaps by imports), higher food subsidies will drive up the food price more than proportionately to limit demand, offsetting their intended effect.[7]

The moral is that if output adjusts to meet demand in stagnationist fashion, stabilization programmes are not incompatible with modestly progressive income redistribution. However, the rules change when economic activity nears the upper bounds

[7] The more than proportionate response occurs because the extra subsidies are equivalent to a fiscal injection, adding to overall aggregate demand which must be limited by forced saving.

imposed by available productive capacity or foreign exchange. The paradox of thrift goes some way towards explaining the failures of stabilization-*cum*- redistribution in Chile under Allende in the early 1970s, in Argentina when progressive redistribution in 1973–75 fed into inflation and crisis by 1976, and in Brazil with the failure of a wage–price freeze coupled with redistribution in 1986.

The next step is to extend the analysis to economies with more than one sector. But before going on it makes sense to summarize the discussion to this point. In terms of their adjustments to perturbations, one can distinguish between macroeconomic models which rely on substitution effects (mainly neoclassical in spirit and formulation) and those built around income changes (mainly proposed by structuralists). The former are likely to generate exhilarationist responses, the latter stagnationist, in the terminology defined above. Structural models further can be built around changes in the level or distribution of income. Some shocks, for example austerity when there is excess capacity, mainly affect income levels. Others, for example an attempt at progressive redistribution at full capacity, almost exclusively influence income shares. A third class of macro changes may affect output and distribution simultaneously. We will see in the next section, for example, that devaluation may provoke recession by forcing regressive shifts in the income distribution. To repeat a theme stressed throughout this essay, the practical relevance of these different models depends on the conditions at hand. Neither neoclassical nor structural linkages universally apply.

Turning to models with more than one sector, the first point to observe is that such disaggregations are set up by practitioners on the basis of their perceptions of key institutional differences between parts of the economy. In developing countries, sectors with different production structures and/or relationships to foreign trade are often separated for further analysis. Three two-sector models are briefly described here, one based on the distinction between agriculture and industry and two emphasizing the different macroeconomic roles of effectively traded and non-traded goods. All show up in the WIDER country studies.[8]

---

[8] Another common distinction is between sectors producing capital and consumer goods. This break-down is more relevant to the analysis of medium-run growth than stabilization, and is not taken up here.

In a macro model with several sectors, output and forced saving adjustment processes can interact in complex fashion. One or more sectors may reach equilibrium through changes in quantities (output or occasionally exports or imports of nationally produced or very similar commodities), and others by movements in prices. Our first example is based on the observation that markets for foods and staples often clear through price changes, or would do so in the absence of active state intervention. In the jargon, such sectors are characterized by 'flex-prices'. In practice, flex-price movements are usually regulated by the state via support schemes, food subsidies, variable levies on external trade, and so on. The reason is that both demand and supply elasticities for staples are low, making extreme fluctuations in their uncontrolled prices inevitable. Farmers and food consumers are politically sensitive groups: most governments dread offending either and opt for trying to hold prices steady for both. But the interventions only soften and do not overcome intrinsic market instability. They can also prove very expensive, as food subsidies recently amounting to tens of per cents of fiscal outlay in Sri Lanka and Egypt illustrate.

By contrast to staples, industrial products often have administered or mark-up prices. We arrive at a 'fix/flex' classification of price adjustment used in most of the country studies, with agricultural prices varying and industrial prices stable (though in war-torn Nicaragua and dollar-starved Tanzania traditionally marked-up prices for urban and industrial goods turned increasingly flex). On the quantity side, agricultural output is fixed in the short run while industrial output is determined by demand. We have a mixture of our two one-sector adjustment mechanisms.[9]

Several observations about how this model (and by extension, a real economy) works can be made immediately. Any demand injection will bid up both food prices and non-food output. Therefore the agricultural terms-of-trade will be positively related to the level of economic activity. By cutting real wages, higher food prices can trigger a structural inflation if the appropriate propagation mechanisms are present, as discussed in Section 2.1

---

[9] The two-sector model sketched in the text keeps being reinvented; representative presentations include Kalecki (1965), Kaldor (1976), Okun (1981), Taylor (1983), and Sylos-Labini (1984). The fix-price/flex-price terminology is due to Hicks (1965).

The terms-of-trade also figure in a distributional question that has been around at least since the early nineteenth century when Malthus and Ricardo debated the effects of repealing the British Corn Laws. Will higher food prices cause demand for industrial products to rise or fall? In a three-sector extension of the model, what about better prices for export crops?

The answers depend on a balance of forces. Richer food-producing farmers will certainly buy more goods, but at the same time urban-dwellers' real incomes decline with rising food prices. They may cut their industrial purchases sharply back, especially if demand for agricultural commodities is highly income-inelastic (as Engel's Law suggests). Malthus, a defender of landlord interests, argued that a positive industrial response to higher agricultural prices was likely. National spending patterns seem to verify his prediction in contemporary Sri Lanka and India; when export crop receipts are taken into consideration, the same observation applies to Tanzania as well. A negative aggregate demand response to higher food prices may be the rule in Turkey, Argentina, Colombia, and Nicaragua. However, foreign exchange restrictions also have to be taken into account. Better export prices may ease external strangulation in Nicaragua and elsewhere; higher food prices cut import requirements by stimulating supply and offsetting stagflation in Tanzania in 1975–78 and very recently in Peru. All these examples suggest that intersectoral distributional relationships in developing countries can have significant macroeconomic effects. They can make orthodox policies aimed at getting agricultural prices higher or 'right' politically very difficult to implement.

Another fix/flex system involves tradable and non-tradable goods, with the distinction resulting from transport costs and trade policy. Some importables may have their supplies fixed by quotas, for example, and as a consequence have freely varying internal prices. Privileged importers with access to the quotas reap a margin between the border price (world price × exchange rate) and the internal price of the goods under the quota. Will allowing more imports into the economy stimulate or retard aggregate demand via distributional shifts? The question has recently been studied theoretically,[10] and figures in the WIDER papers. The answer, at

---

[10] For example, by Barbone (1985) and Ocampo (1987a).

least recently in Mexico and Colombia, is that liberalizing import quotas makes the internal level of activity decline. An effective quota system in Kenya may have contributed to keeping output in that externally shocked economy up. Further questions revolve around the effects of devaluation when there are quotas, and are taken up in Section 3.2.

The third price/quantity story hinges on the flexibility of prices of non-traded goods as aggregate demand changes, say from a foreign exchange bonanza. The adjustment scenario sketched in Section 2.2 is based on upward pressure against non-traded prices (including wages when labour markets are tight) under an attack of Dutch disease. It is relevant for Egypt and Mexico in the 1970s. In the opposite direction, relatively falling non-tradable prices (and wages) under austerity augmented by incomes policies and devaluation show up in several countries, including Mexico in the 1980s, Kenya, Chile, and Turkey. Only in Turkey was depreciation of the 'real' exchange rate (defined as the ratio of traded to non-traded goods' prices) associated with much of a trade response. It is argued below that the Turkish export boom owed more to prior industrial investment and favourable external market conditions than to relative price shifts.

A final topic under the heading of macro adjustment is the relationship among components of total commodity production or demand (which could be further linked with distributional changes and supply shocks). Six important linkages are brought out in the country papers.

First, demand patterns may shift unexpectedly, especially under big movements in the inflation rate or when foreign debt and capital flight are substantial. Several examples involve devaluation. The increase in the local value of externally held assets that devaluation causes may stimulate consumer purchasers (as in Mexico in recent years). On the other hand, firms with dollar liabilities will see their balance sheets deteriorate abruptly; unless bailed out by state intervention, they may be driven into bankruptcy with strong recessionary consequences.[11] Tracing through such effects can be complex. The situation is made even more obscure by the presence

---

[11] Fisher (1933) proposed a 'debt-deflation' theory of depressions along such lines. As discussed in Chapter 4, such balance-sheet collapses have threatened from time to time in South Korea, but have been offset by massive state-backed credit injections.

of the state. If it is responsible for paying external debt (the usual case), devaluation increases the local currency value of its foreign obligations. Tax increases to meet the government's nominally greater interest and amortization bill would make real output contract. On the other hand, if the government borrows from the central bank to meet the local counterpart of its dollar obligations, its action increases base money in the same quantity as foreign outflow cuts it back by reducing reserves. To a first approximation, local state borrowing to meet external obligations is neutral in monetary (and aggregate demand) terms. Similar effects are caused by changes in the inflation rate, as discussed in Section 3.4. In practice, forecasting the direction in which demand propensities will move under a major stabilization is next to impossible, since they respond to so many forces. Art in policy design is essential at this point.

The second demand connection is between public and private investment. Does capital formation by the central government or public enterprises crowd private investment in or out? Orthodoxy postulates crowding-out under unchanging monetary policy. The government borrows to finance its projects, absorbing credit and bidding up interest rates. As a consequence private investment falls. The WIDER authors recognize this financial effect, but uniformly stress another on the real side of the system. There appear to be strong complementarities between public and private capital formation in the mixed economies that most developing countries have evolved, so that government projects (ideally of good quality) stimulate entrepreneurs. When this linkage operates, austerity-imposed cuts in public investment will be doubly contractionary because they will make private capital spending fall as well. In the recent period, the effect seems especially strong in the Ivory Coast, Egypt, Turkey, Mexico, Argentina, and (on the up side) Brazil.

The third example involves domestic demand ('absorption' in the jargon) and exports. In some economies there appears to be a greater vent for surplus sales abroad if internal purchases of the relevant commodities are held down. This absorption/export trade-off shows up in two contexts. One is in middle-income countries which have broken away from specialization in primary commodity exports (internal demand for which is often small and stable) and have a manufacturing base in place. Examples among the WIDER countries include Turkey, Mexico, Argentina, Brazil, and Korea. There may also be a trade-off if a country predominately exports its 'wage good'—historical examples are Argentine beef and Thai rice—or if export and food crops are close technical substitutes in production. In either case, there is a potential conflict between output growth and trade improvement—a difficult dilemma to resolve.

Fourth, production substitution between export crops and food has implications for price policy, an important form of state intervention. If the relative export-crop/food-crop price is increased in an attempt to generate foreign exchange, then domestic food supply may drop off. The consequent inflation makes avoiding overvaluation to sustain exports all the more difficult. This compositional problem (like the one taken up next) became chronic in small, poor developing economies when primary commodity prices broke downwards around 1976.

Fifth, in an externally strangled economy a contradiction between capital formation and economic activity arises when both investment and output require imported goods. To an extent, investment pressure on scarce foreign exchange (directly, and indirectly through intermediate imports) can be 'resolved' by forced saving. But either through that price mechanism or via state control, increased capital formation necessarily crowds out domestic production when the foreign constraint binds.[12]

Finally, there is much to be said for fiscal prudence. The public deficit should be kept low enough to avoid driving the economy against output limits and bringing in forced saving or the inflation tax mode of macroeconomic adjustment discussed in Section 3.4 below. However, tax revenue losses and spending increases may be imposed upon the state for diverse reasons. The more common include political instability, the need to offset external shocks or supply losses from natural disasters, foreign payment obligations (discussed above and in Section 3.3), and financial outlays such as bail-outs of the banking system after a collapse or monetary

---

[12] Typical import contents in the sub-Saharan African context might be 60 per cent for investment and 20 per cent for the rest of GDP, with an overall average of 30 per cent. Under such conditions, an increase in current output sharply cuts back on capacity formation. See Green and Kadhani (1986) for such calculations as applied to Zimbabwe.

indexation involving interest payments on state debt (Section 3.4). At the same time, upper bounds on output may shift down, from disasters (again), insufficient investment in the immediate past, or a dearth of foreign exchange. Fiscal imbalance is an aspect of many shocks that has to be stabilized. It is not often the primary destabilizing factor, despite orthodox assertions to the contrary.[13]

3.2 Price–Cost Relationships

Considering distributional effects on aggregate demand has already led us into the maze of feedbacks between prices and costs. In this section, we take up further linkages emphasized in the WIDER papers. The catalogue is not complete on a world scale, but keeping even price–cost relationships applicable to developing countries in order will be a page-consuming task. We begin with a general discussion of price formation rules, going on to take up mark-up rates, wage dynamics, costs of imported inputs (plus controversial questions about the effects of devaluation), working capital costs, pricing of nationally produced intermediate inputs (often provided by public enterprises), and indirect taxes.

At the outset, a central question about pricing centres around model closure or causality. Is a sector's price level determined by independent production input prices? Or does it vary on its own, thereby determining some component of cost? Mark-up pricing, where the price level = mark-up rate × prime cost, is an example of the first sort of relationship.[14] Sectors in which a flexible market price moves up or down to bring demand and supply into balance represent the second. Price per unit output decomposes into costs—wages, purchases of intermediate inputs, interest on working capital, and operating surpluses. In flex-price sectors, one or more

[13] Sachs (1987) vigorously presents the orthodox case against fiscal imprudence and reliance on the inflation tax. He does not consider shifts in the income distribution and forced saving, the income flow counterparts of the real wealth stock changes underlying changes in saving propensities induced by inflation. In practice, both flow and stock variations are likely to be of policy concern.

[14] 'Prime cost' here means the cost of short-run variable inputs per unit of output. There is a huge literature devoted to microeconomic justifications for mark-up pricing rules, which represents too much of a diversion to be pursued here. Kalecki (1971) and Sylos-Labini (1984) contain the basic insights.

of these components must accommodate when output prices vary. We take up the possibilities *seriatim*, and then move on to mark-up pricing.

As we have already noted, the classic flex-prices are for primary commodities—exports in the world market and foodstuffs within the national economy. Diverse income flows respond to their fluctuations. With farms typically run by families, for example, it is hard to separate their returns to capital and labour costs. An upward swing in farm prices of staple goods adds to 'farm income' after costs of hired-in labour, intermediates, and finance are deducted. Traders add an element of cost between the farm and consumer food prices, and their margins may rise and fall substantially as supply conditions change (especially in sub-Saharan Africa). At times, some such element of cost may suffer from a downward price swing. Wages of non-Ivorian migrant workers in the Ivory Coast could be an example. Analogous buffers appear elsewhere in the economy. Public enterprise prices may be regulated, with the state's profit income absorbing changes. In services, incomes of family enterprises and some of their workers go up and down. The point is that when prices are free to move, a residual element (or elements) in the producers' input accounts must have its level endogenously determined.

When we leave flex-price markets it becomes straightforward to think in terms of mark-up pricing (or, for the neoclassically inclined, cost functions). Final prices are set by input costs for labour and intermediates, along with the mark-up. Six theories about how margins are determined show up in the WIDER papers.

First, the price level may be set by the money supply, as in the equation of exchange discussed in Section 2.1. How monetarists square this theory with the decomposition of price into costs is never quite clear. One approach is to deny the existence of pure profits in full employment perfect competition, and to assume that all nominal prices rise proportionately in response to an increase in the money supply. Less mystically (or more realistically), producers' incomes may be the adjusting variable, obeying the rule mark-up rate = price level/prime cost. This equation leaves no room for cost-push elements in inflation. Given the money supply, higher costs (including, but not solely, wages) just reduce margins.

This can be taken as an extreme monetarist position, stated but not endorsed in the WIDER studies.[15]

The second option is to suppose that the mark-up rate depends directly on the money supply, so that the price level is affected by both monetary conditions and costs. This is the theory in the papers on the Ivory Coast, Tanzania, and Sri Lanka. Rapid growth in money is said to signal a strong injection of demand from the fiscal deficit, and final commodity prices respond. Presumably other forms of demand injection (higher private investment, say) would give the same result, so that macro adjustment occurs along flex-price, forced-saving lines. The implicit limits on output come from scarce foreign exchange and/or basic food commodities.

Third, other papers take a less roundabout approach, postulating that the mark-up (or its rate of change) in industrial sectors depends directly on the level of economic activity. In Colombia, the level of the mark-up appears to vary pro-cyclically; perhaps it moves weakly against the cycle in Brazil. Both reactions show up in price equations estimated around the world, along with a more common result that mark-up rates stay essentially stable (the case in the WIDER papers for Argentina, Mexico, and elsewhere).

Fourth, mark-ups may rise in response to specific bottle necks. Examples are low food supply (bringing us back towards flex-price stories), an inelastic supply of home goods in a foreign exchange glut, or unavailable essential imports in a foreign exchange dearth. This last shortfall lay behind the accelerations of inflation in several countries after dollar shortages arose in the late 1970s.

Fifth, foreign competition may affect internal prices, for example making mark-ups decline in response to import liberalization. This effect is orthodox, a modest but practical manifestation of the law of one price discussed in Section 2.2. It is accorded varying degrees of

[15] The strictly inverse trade-off between the real wage and the profit rate implicit in our interpretation of monetarists' models is not unique to them. In the realm of economic theory it recurs in full employment neoclassical stories, Marxist formulations which assert that a higher wage (due, perhaps, to depletion of the reserve army) holds down profits and retards accumulation, and Sraffa's (1960) critique of neoclassical theory. The contrast with the stagnationist model discussed above—where both the wage bill and the profit rate can rise in an economic expansion—is striking, and shows up in allegedly practical pronouncements from members of the various schools. In a stylized model for Mexico, Gibson, Lustig, and Taylor (1986) present numerical simulations to illustrate the point.

empirical support in the country papers (perhaps the most in Tanzania and Peru). A degree of recession for domestic producers may accompany the inflation slow-down.

Sixth, as already noted, the mark-up rate may remain relatively stable, but subject to shocks from any of the factors mentioned above or other political or economic events. With a constant mark-up, the rate of price inflation in the relevant sectors decomposes into a weighted average of rates of inflation of wages, intermediate input costs (which in turn break down largely into costs of inputs from public enterprises and imported goods with internal prices affected by the exchange rate and world market conditions), interest rate increases which make working capital more expensive to finance, and changes in indirect tax rates. When flex-price variations are added to the equation with appropriate weights, one has an explanation of the overall inflation rate. This is a structuralist formulation, exemplified in WIDER papers for countries (especially in Latin America) where there is a long history of entrenched inflation. Structuralism directs attention to the forces determining the growth rates of costs, the topic we take up next.

The major element is the wage bill. When indexed, wages are usually tied to past inflation, a magnitude known to all. Structuralists argue that backward-looking indexation is rational under inflation. All economic actors can agree upon it, avoiding unpleasant surprises and reducing transactions costs. Forward-looking indexation has been tried occasionally, for example in Brazil in the late 1960s and Mexico in the 1980s, but tends to break down because governments and/or the Fund rarely resist the temptation to underestimate future inflation. Official economic projections look rosy and public sector real outlays—projected in normal terms—are held down, but workers protest about the real wage losses created by nominal increases based upon an understated price inflation rate.

When there is indexation, an upward jump in prices, by causing the real wage to fall, can lead to wage increases which are passed along into further price increases through the mark-up, and so on. Such a sequence represents a classical structural inflation: the initial price shock can of course be caused by a number of factors. The inflation will be faster as the 'pass-through' of lagged price increases into wage increases approaches (or exceeds) 100 per cent, and the readjustment period shortens. Under three-digit annual inflation upward wage revisions may occur quarterly, or even more often. Such wage-indexation rules (plus analagous treatment of the exchange rate in a 'crawling peg' tied to past inflation) make the overall rate of price increase highly sensitive to upward shocks. In orthodox stabilizations, reduced pass-through proportions, stretched-out indexation periods, or both, often appear. They produce a fall in real wages. If the economy behaves in stagnationist fashion on a downswing, aggregate demand and the level of activity will also fall. 'Heterodox shocks' as applied in Latin America in the 1980s try to evade these problems by de-indexing the economy at a stroke. This approach is discussed more fully in Section 3.4 below.

Factors besides past inflation obviously affect wage dynamics. Extreme recession, by enlarging reserve armies, can make labour less aggressive. When successful, monetarist stabilizations slow inflation from the side of costs by creating unemployment through austerity. Genuinely accepted or highly repressive regimes may achieve better control over wages than unpopular or merely nasty ones. But under politically and economically 'normal' circumstances, a downward jump in the real wage from unanticipated inflation is likely to lead to labour cost pressure. One common cause is a major or maxi-devaluation, the topic we take up next.

Intermediate imports comprise a large proportion of prime cost in developing countries, nearly as much as labour on a national basis when domestic intermediates are netted out.[16] Devaluation increases import costs, which under mark-up rules soon pass into higher prices. This inflationary effect is emphasized in almost all the country studies. The resulting cuts in the real wage and aggregate demand are also frequently mentioned. In the jargon, they make devaluation contractionary.

There are additional linkages leading to the same result. Depreciation when there is an existing trade deficit gives with one hand by increasing export revenues, but takes more with the other in terms of higher import costs. There is an overall national income loss in local currency terms; hence contraction. Exchange rate

[16] Typical proportions of wages and intermediate import costs to GDP might be 30–50 and 20–40 per cent respectively in a small, open, developing economy. The wage ratio is lower than in industrialized economies because a large share of value-added accrues to independent proprietors like peasants and traders.

changes also act as an element of fiscal policy. Devaluation increases nominal tariff receipts, which may comprise a large share of total tax revenues. In agro-exporting economies, overseas sales often go through marketing boards which buy from farmers internally and turn around to sell their crops abroad. With such a set-up, devaluation increases local currency export receipts in the hands of the marketing boards. Unless the extra revenue is passed along to government spending Ministries or producer households with high marginal propensities to consume, it is not injected into the system and economic activity thereby declines. In view of these linkages, the contemporary consensus in the WIDER (and other developing country) macro studies is that devaluation causes short-run stagflation—inflation and output contraction at the same time.[17]

When it is present, contractionary devaluation has important policy implications. Analysis of potential trade-offs helps illustrate the issues involved. Suppose the goal is to improve external balance while maintaining a constant level of capacity utilization by some combination of devaluation and austerity. Both depreciation and a reduced demand injection increase the trade surplus. If devaluation is expansionary, its effect on output will be offset by demand reduction. Hence austerity and depreciation can be combined. On the other hand, if devaluation is contractionary it has to be put together with expansionary policy to keep activity constant. Orthodox stabilizations usually include both depreciation and austerity. When devaluation is contractionary, orthodox packages are wide open to the common accusation that they embody macroeconomic 'overkill'.

Forces counteracting contraction should be mentioned. First, there are the wealth effects brought up in Section 3.1, which may increase consumer or public sector demand.

Second, price-induced import substitution and export growth due to higher traded goods prices make devaluation less contrac-

[17] Contractionary impacts of devaluation are an old theme in the structuralist tradition. Diaz-Alejandro (1963) pointed out the real wage effect, which works in the same way as forced saving. Hirschman (1949) was the first to note that contraction is likely with a pre-existing trade deficit. Cooper (1971) discusses the political economy of devaluation. Krugman and Taylor (1978) pull much of this literature together, and mention the fiscal effects discussed in the text.

tionary (or perhaps expansionary) with a lag.[18] But while these volume changes are unfolding, real depreciation from a maxi-devaluation is likely to be eroding from structural inflation as workers seek to recover pre-devaluation levels of real wages. Which effect will win the race is by no means certain. In Colombia in the 1950s and 1960s there were three-year cycles beginning with a maxi, then an export push, real appreciation and export stagnation, and a maxi again. The policy response in that country was the invention of the 'crawling peg' where the nominal exchange rate is depreciated at the domestic inflation rate (less world inflation) to hold the real exchange rate constant. Mexico went through an old-fashioned Colombian episode in 1983–85. Real appreciation under structural inflation occurred when its crawl was slowed for fear of 'excessive' monetary expansion due to a reserve build-up as the balance of payments improved. Ancient policy mistakes have a way of repeating themselves.

A third observation is that arguments in support of contractionary devaluation make most sense when the level of activity is determined from the demand side. If output is strictly constrained by available import capacity, then any move that generates foreign exchange is likely to bring an output increase together with slower inflation as forced saving eases off. Devaluation will not reduce import coefficients by much in the short run, but it could generate a modest export response (say an elasticity of 0.25 or so over the first year, increasing thereafter). Even that would help the level of activity by admitting more intermediate imports into the system.

Fourth and finally, the importance of contractionary and expansionary effects depends on policy and institutions. For example, in Nigeria (not one of the WIDER countries) two-fifths of revenues from oil exports are mandated to state and local governments by the constitution. Since the propensity to consume of these entities can safely be assumed to be one, devaluation by increasing local currency oil receipts gives a strong expansionary kick.[19]

---

[18] These responses are called 'J-curves' in the literature, after the (vague) resemblance between the letter J and a plot of foreign currency export revenues against time. Revenues drop at the point of devaluation, because the same volume of local exports costs less abroad, and then gradually increase as volume rises in response to lower prices.

[19] For details in a model simulation, see Taylor, Yurukoglu, and Chaudhry (1986).

Similar scenarios occur in agro-export economies. Suppose that the exchange rate is held constant with an ongoing inflation. To maintain real returns for export-crop producers at a remunerative level, the marketing boards will have to bid up internal prices by running losses. If these are covered by higher taxes, recession becomes likely. Inflation causes real appreciation here, but the feedback through the marketing boards makes the situation worse. Going the other way, sterilization of incremental receipts by marketing boards under devaluation can create contraction, as we have seen. The implication is that the boards cannot operate independently of exchange rate decisions, which is an important institutional constraint. In practice one has to be clear about both economic and institutional reactions before making strong statements about the likely effects of devaluation. *A fortiori* this observation applies to the usual orthodox presumption that currency depreciation creates conditions for non-inflationary output growth.

Considering the inflationary effects of devaluation specifically, a recently popular counter-argument bears discussion. It rests on import quotas, universally acknowledged to be widespread. In the flex-price/fix-price model discussed in Section 3.1, firms holding rights to quotas can make a profit by buying cheap at the border, and then reselling their imports in a tight domestic market. In principle, devaluation should just eat into these 'quota rents', not creating cost pressure.[20] The consequent claim (made most forcibly for African economies) is that exchange depreciation will not drive the price level up.

The problem with this line of reasoning is that it does not go far enough. Suppose devaluation works the way it is supposed to, rapidly stimulating exports and adding to overall demand. If there are rising supply curves in the economy, the outcome would be higher prices along the lines of mark-up theories one to four discussed above. Such an outcome would be more likely in so far as savings rates from quota rents are high—the reduction in rents from

---

[20] We unrealistically ignore the possibility that quota-rentiers might have enough market power to pass increased costs from devaluation along to internal prices. To the extent that this phenomenon occurs (as it seems to do in some WIDER countries), macro responses will more closely approximate the model of contraction discussed previously in the text.

devaluation would not cut demand by much. On the basis of fairly orthodox reasoning of this sort, simple algebraic models show that devaluation will only be price-deflationary if it is output-contractionary as well (Taylor 1987b). One has to eat the contraction frosting along with the anti-inflation cake.

A third component of cost is for working capital. Typically, credit from the banking system to the 'enterprise' sector (including both private and public productive firms) amounts to a quarter of GDP and perhaps half of that goes to finance working capital. Under fast inflation with loan interest rates approaching three-digit percentage levels per year, the share of nominal costs made up of interest payments will be in the range of 10–20 per cent of GDP. Firms will be strongly tempted to pass interest rate increases along into prices. The upshot can be stagflation. Restrictive monetary policy is almost always contractionary because it cuts back demand. It can also be inflationary when working capital is an important element of cost. The effect is well-known.[21] It is said to be empirically important in the papers for Tanzania, the Ivory Coast, Argentina (apparently it was stronger in the late 1970s than later), South Korea, and Brazil.

Another big component of costs comprises nationally produced or processed intermediates, which can be understood properly only when inter-industry linkages among sectors are taken into account. Many of the relevant producers are publically owned in developing countries, and the effects of changes in public enterprise pricing policy become macroeconomically important.

One example in Egypt and elsewhere is petroleum products made and sold nationally at less than world market cost (at least prior to 1986!). Raising internal energy prices resembles devaluation. Cost structures shift upwards in user industries, possibly leading to an overall price increase and contraction (Choucri and Lahiri 1984). At the same time, the energy-saving substitution that higher oil prices are supposed to promote may be slow or require massive investment to reshape existing technologies towards lower energy

---

[21] In the North Atlantic literature, it is called after Wright Patman, a famous easy-money Congressman from Texas. Latins ascribe the effect to Cavallo (1977), although it was noted two decades before by Galbraith (1957) and Streeten and Balogh (1957). Morley (1971) presents an early empirical discussion from Brazil.

use. The same general considerations apply to other price revisions aimed at inducing greater economic efficiency.

Further complications arise. If price revisions make domestic production costs go up, devaluation may be required to restore external competitiveness. From a monetarist perspective, raising prices charged by public firms should increase their operating surpluses and shrink fiscal subsidies, thereby reducing state borrowing from the central bank. The gain from lower inflation due to less money creation has to be offset against the cost pressure that higher public sector prices create. The net result is not obvious, and has been debated in India and elsewhere in recent years.[22]

The conclusion is that the macroeconomic implications of state enterprise management can be important in some contexts, and have to be carefully considered. This observation should not be construed as an argument for capricious public sector pricing. Rather it implies that there are both costs and benefits to price revision (even ignoring political considerations). There are no magical outcomes to be expected from getting publicly controlled prices higher, lower, or even 'right'.

Finally, on the fiscal side, changes in indirect tax or tariff rates will alter cost structures and thereby prices. Since direct taxes typically account for a small share of revenues in developing countries, this effect is practically important. In several WIDER countries, for example Mexico and Brazil, attempts to raise state revenues have proven to be inflationary through the cost–price linkage.

3.3 The Balance of Payments

A great deal has already been said about how different components of the balance of payments respond to policy, so only the main points are summarized in this section. We begin with interventions aimed principally at the merchandise trade account (austerity, devaluation, liberalization), proceed to capital market complications, and close with observations about factors influencing trade in services.

[22] Computable general equilibrium model simulations for India by Sarkar and Panda (1986) suggest that the cost pressures dominate the reduction in mark-ups induced by tighter money. Maasland (1987) gets similar results in a model for Sri Lanka.

Under orthodox stabilization, the main tools affecting commodity and service transactions are austerity and devaluation. Austere programmes often 'work' in the sense of making the trade balance improve. But they succeed by reducing output and capital formation (both with high import contents) rather than by promoting import substitution or export promotion. Devaluation suffers the same drawbacks—it helps the trade balance mostly by contraction in the short run. However, exchange rate movements also have longer term effects, some involving improvements in the tradability of domestic products. The plot of the devaluation story is not easy to unravel.

The first twist is simply the fact that depreciation is unpleasant from the moment it occurs. Avoiding the pain makes appreciation look attractive: it may cut inflation and stimulate production for a time. Unfortunately, other problems arise. An externally strong (or overvalued) currency worsens the trade account; it can put potential export and import substitution activities out of business in short order. Also, a strong rate seeds its own destruction. Capital inflow set off by an import-led boom can support a trade deficit at first. But as the external gap remains and local tradable goods production falters, pressures for a maxi-devaluation—the 'obvious' policy response—intensify. Exchange controls cease to deter capital flight in anticipation of the local windfall gain the maxi will bring; bank reserves fall. The inevitable stabilization may combine the worst measures that can be imposed: austerity, wage-cutting, and depreciation *à outrance*. Mexico, the Philippines, and the Southern Cone all illustrate this sequence of events. The only beneficiaries were exchange rate speculators whose placement of assets abroad was stabilization's proximate cause.

Second, one has to consider other policies connected with successful exchange rate manoeuvres. In some WIDER studies trade gains were linked with devaluation: import substitution of rice in Sri Lanka and capital goods in Brazil, and export growth in Brazil, Turkey, South Korea, and Colombia. In all these cases, however, the improvements had their way paved by prior or concurrent investment (often by the public sector) which created the needed capacity. The capital formation was surely necessary for increased production of traded goods.[23] Shifting relative prices to stimulate 'tradability' no doubt helped the process along. But whether devaluation or more directed price incentives were essential is another question. Even if they were, overall depreciation was not necessarily the wisest policy choice. Its economy-wide effects—contraction and inflation—suggest prudence if the exchange rate is roughly on line. They wreak havoc when it is not.

The moral is that a relatively weak exchange rate is necessary to avoid the perils of overvaluation, and may be instrumental (along with other factors) in achieving medium-run trade improvement without stagflation. These are good reasons not to have the exchange rate 'wrong', but if it is not strongly overvalued there is not much of a case for maxi-devaluations aimed at setting it right. The country studies support this last point, along with its corollary that extreme appreciation, always a risk under inflation, should be studiously avoided. A crawling peg roughly indexed to the continuing inflation is a sensible policy for keeping trade relationships on an even keel (although if financial markets are dollarized it may feed back into higher local interest rates). The rate of crawl can always be manipulated at the margin to create a bit of depreciation or appreciation if real exchange rate corrections seem in order.

Besides devaluation, trade liberalization often shows up in orthodox packages. The moves seem at cross-purposes: one is supposed to narrow the trade gap but the other makes it wider. Moreover, the widening can come in socially dubious fashion. In Tanzania, Ghana, Sri Lanka, and Argentina a substantial share of new imports after trade barriers were lowered took the form of consumer goods instead of capital goods or intermediates. Domestic productive activity, except in the import-handling service sectors, was not enhanced. If a process of income concentration is underway—as was the case in some of the countries that practised liberalization—letting in more consumer imports satisfies the changes in demand composition implicit in the distributional shift.

---

[23] An exception to this rule may be Ghana, where devaluation was undertaken in connection with an orthodox stabilization backed by ample external balance of payments support. The official rate had previously been thousands of per cent overvalued, so that giving it a realistic value added order to a chaotic system and no doubt brought a large share of external transactions from parallel markets to the official one.

But liberalization does not stimulate domestic production of 'luxuries', so that even the manufacturing thrust that regressive income redistribution can create is blunted. From this perspective it is hard to see what improvements liberalization may bring.

Advocates point to three advantages. The first—conjunctural—is that removing trade barriers is anti-inflationary. We have already noted (Section 3.2) that this notion lacks decisive empirical support, while theoretical arguments in its favour are hard to mount with the law of one price in abeyance.

The second gain from liberalization is secular: according to numerous theorems of neoclassical economics, production and efficiency rise when distortions are removed. The theory is not uniformly supported by evidence from the WIDER sample. 'Success' cases such as South Korea, Brazil, and Turkey are scarcely historical paragons of liberal policy; extreme anti-distortionist regimes were associated with macroeconomic disaster in the Southern Cone and current stagnation in Mexico and elsewhere. On the other hand, restoring order by removing impediments to official markets no doubt contributed (along with ample capital inflows) to orthodox stabilization's success in the mid-1980s in Ghana. These examples suggest that although liberalization is attractive intellectually to mainstream economists, its usefulness in practice depends on the circumstances. And surely, in the short run, rapid dismantlement of barriers to trade (and capital movements) can create payments problems like a shot.

Third, no one doubts that quantitative restrictions go hand-in-hand with intrusive bureaucracies, wasteful rent-seeking, and so on. Retaliation on the part of trading partners to import restraints and export subsidies is known to occur. A question of rising costs and decreasing benefits to trade intervention arises, with the slopes and positions of the curves highly dependent on context.

The WIDER country papers emphasize the potential gains from directed interventions: import quotas, export subsidies, and a differential commercial policy regime all around. Quotas may be expansionary (as, for example, in Colombia and Kenya). They give quick responses, which can be administratively advantageous in many situations. Subsidies may be necessary to make exports flow, and are likely to be less disruptive macroeconomically than maxi-devaluation. Such policies are widely pursued in practice, and seem unlikely to be abandoned. The sensible course might be to think about how to make them more effective in stimulating production and satisfying consumers' desires. If undertaken, liberalization exercises should proceed along lines of common sense.

Turning to the capital account, a major argument in favour of austerity when embodied in Fund/Bank programmes is that it opens doors for new loans from abroad. The extra dollars are supposed to make reasonable growth rates possible after a liberalization/stabilization hiatus.[24] As we have already noted, both statements tend in the direction of truth, but only partly.

The main favourable examples in our sample are Ghana, Turkey, and Sri Lanka in the 1980s, and the boom period in Chile a bit before. All these countries engaged in import-led growth under liberalizing regimes, with much of the foreign cover for their trade deficits coming from official sources. This ploy can only last so long: as recounted in Chapter 4, Chile's boom soon bust, while more recently Ghana's debt service obligations have been mounting ominously (to 55–60 per cent of exports). The WIDER sample also includes countries pursuing orthodox tacks which did not receive additional capital—Kenya and the Ivory Coast come to mind. Even if 'new money' is liberated by orthodoxy, the package need not generate successful stabilization: Mexico in the 1980s and protracted poor performance in the Philippines under two decades of IMF tutelage stand out. And finally, adjustment can occur under fairly heterodox packages: Colombia, Argentina, South Korea, and Peru.

The implication seems to be that although austerity warms financiers' hearts, it does not always open their coffers. Successful anti-austerity might prove a better skeleton key. The incentives from abroad for standard policy packages arguably exist; the question is how generous in a given situation the reward for conformity will be.

The second major topic on capital account refers to the actions of nationals. Under what circumstances will they engage in capital flight? It seems clear from the record that speculation against future devaluation of an overvalued exchange rate is the major cause for

---

[24] Tiding a country over the short-run difficulties of liberalization is viewed as the major justification for external assistance by a prominent functionary of the World Bank (see Lal 1987).

flight, but any loss of confidence in the regime can set it off. The countermeasures, as usual, are carrots and sticks.

The main inducements to keep money at home are institutional: the Brazilian bourgeoisie probably engages in less flight than its counterparts elsewhere because it has traditionally concentrated on industrial rather than commercial activity. But such attitudes only solidify with time. For the shorter term, typical policy instruments aimed at slowing flight include a high interest rate, and a weak exchange rate kept undervalued in real terms by a crawling peg. The effect of both policies on investment by local firms is not likely to be favourable. Indeed, they may be tempted to borrow abroad in such a situation. With high rates, both the arriving capital and domestic savings flows will have difficulty finding outlets in the form of real capital formation. Low levels of commodity production (though not necessarily services) could be one consequence; active markets in financial assets and/or real estate another. Financial speculators flower in such a garden: recall the example of Chile discussed in Section 2.1.

Another incentive against capital flight takes the form of local currency financial instruments indexed to the exchange rate and paying attractive interest rates. Many countries have invented such paper, first for fiscal and subsequently private debt. Occasionally these assets go too far in masquerading as foreign. The run against and subsequent buy-out of Mex-dollars in 1982 is a case in point. Another showed up in Egypt in the mid-1980s where 'real' dollar deposits in banks became increasingly hollow as the government tapped the reserves to pay for imports under impending external strangulation. The consensus in the WIDER papers seems to be that local dollar or dollar-denominated assets can be useful stabilizers for modest fluctuations in the capital market, but do not provide much defence against big movements (either private or engineered by state actions).

A last foil against adverse capital flows is exchange control—the stick in this particular policy box. Countries in the sample range from having very weak control regimes (the Ivory Coast, the Southern Cone in its liberal period, Nicaragua under the Somozas, Mexico) to fairly strong ones (Brazil, Colombia, South Korea). Those with controls have been less damaged by flight (though the comparison is subject to the inevitable problem of 'holding other factors equal') and their growth record does not seem to have been hindered by their less than liberal policy stance. The problem in recommending it to other countries is that establishing a credible control system is not easy. Investors scan accustomed financial horizons when they consider where to place their portfolios. When they are used to looking abroad it may take years of obstructions to flows and acceptable local returns to make them concentrate their attention at home.[25]

Finally, when capital has fled how does one pick up the pieces? Debt to support the flight may have been contracted by public agencies or the private sector. In the latter case a familiar scenario features foreign obligations of firms expanding simultaneously with deposits held by firm-owners abroad. The build-up of household foreign assets from this sort of capital flight created the 'rich businesmen, poor businesses' of the departing Mexican President Lopez Portillo's (1982) famous lament. As discussed more fully in Section 3.4, governments assumed the liability counterpart of the businessmen's new wealth. With such a bail-out complete, the state must generate a resource flow to meet the external payments due. Two transfers are involved.

The first, familiar from trade theory, is the payment to foreign creditors, requiring a trade surplus. The well-known themes of contraction, devaluation, structural inflation, and so on enter here. The second transfer is internal. Since the government owes the debt and exporters own foreign exchange, it has to buy or tax dollars from them. Coupled with the need to run a trade surplus, this fiscal manoeuvre is not easy to execute in economies under stress. As in the Philippines in the mid-1980s, it can easily prove contractionary as the government attempts to withdraw large sums from the local credit flows to service its foreign debts. The trick becomes even more difficult in countries where the financial system is fragile because of attempts to restructure previous chaos. The more striking examples are described in Section 3.4.

Two last variables involved in balance of payments adjustment are the interest rate and service trade. In an economy more or less

[25] Similar reasoning applies to attempts by developing countries to bring in additional direct foreign investment to help ease balance of payments problems. The 'fundamentals' take a long time to establish: both raising and lowering trade barriers may play a role. Helleiner (1987) provides a review.

open to capital movements, loosely tying the base interest rate to the world market makes common sense. But what range of flexibility for monetary policy does this rule allow? Arida (1986) notes the trade-offs involved. If exchange markets are open, low rates encourage capital flight but will be expansionary by stimulating investment demand. However, high rates may be more destabilizing still. Lustig and Ros (1987) point out that with a pre-existing fiscal debt, high interest costs will force more local borrowing implying a higher deficit, extra debt accumulation, and so on. 'Traps' appear with both low and high rates—capital flight on the one hand versus unsustainable fiscal deficits on the other. The implication is that local rates should be pegged no further above the world market than blocking adverse capital movements entails. In Latin America, especially, this last piece of advice has been taken to an extreme—real rates approach double digits per month. In other parts of the world, negative real rates in local financial markets are the order of the day, raising the spectre of financial repression. How seriously that ghost should be taken is discussed in Section 3.4.

Most poor countries run deficits on non-factor service trade, some components of which (such as tourism) are sensitive to the exchange rate. But such payments are not a central concern for stabilization. Factor services flows—interest and remittances of profits and labour incomes—often are. Interest obligations on external debt (involving flow transfers of several per cent of GDP) have already been discussed as a transfer problem, on the tacit assumption that the transfer will actually take place. Increasingly it does not, as countries run up arrears on foreign debt. Several in the WIDER sample are following this course. One, Peru, has opted for an explicit policy of meeting only part of its foreign obligations. So far it has been able to obtain short-term finance to keep its commodity trade and non-factor service flows in order. The example may spread, but meanwhile in most other countries uncertainty about the status of payments stimulates neither potential foreign investment nor productive spending by local firms.

In other corners of the world remittances are key to any stabilization effort. Sudan, for example, must achieve control over some fraction of remittance inflows generated by emigrant workers if there is to be any financial equilibrium for the state. By liquidating potentially profitable investment projects which could mobilize savings flows, domestic austerity does not help the cause. Elsewhere, remittances flowing outward matter; for example, from both African and non-African expatriate workers in the Ivory Coast. Depending on exchange market conditions, these labour payments plus profit remittances are subject to policies similar to those applied to capital movements. Sticks and carrots shake everywhere, but often ineffectively in the absence of locally credible financial markets and scant possibilities for control of individuals' financial operations by the state. With its capital markets wide open because of its membership in the West African Monetary Union, the Ivory Coast's only tool for cutting remittances from European or non-Ivorian African expatriate workers is to fire them. Other countries in Africa possess the advantage of an inconvertible currency. They can block transfers of expatriates' remittances until they tire of the game, helping the current account but not exactly encouraging new expatriates to come in the future.

3.4 Financial Markets

Financial markets in developing countries clear through complex price and quantity mechanisms, varying across borders and evolving (at times by saltation) over time. Finance has been a focus of stabilization efforts in many of the WIDER countries. Here we take up four issues discussed in several of the studies: macro effects of interest rate changes; the inflation tax and heterodox anti-inflationary shocks; destabilizing interactions between the domestic financial system, the macroeconomy and the world through capital markets; and institutional implications of financial bail-outs.

Four main channels through which the interest rate influences macro adjustment are pointed out in the WIDER papers. First, there is the old idea that rate increases stimulate saving. The benefits of increasing deposit (and presumably lending) rates have recently been urged upon developing countries by the Bank and Fund. A simple neoclassical growth model in which available saving is transformed without hitches to new capital formation underlies the advice, still another example of how model closures pre-determine economists' policy recommendations.[26]

Two sorts of questions immediately arise. First, is the saving effect present, and large enough in quantitative terms to matter? If so, what are the macro implications of more national saving (or what model closure rules really apply)? The evidence on the first query is far from clear. Raising a rate of return to a particular asset (say bank deposits) is likely to induce a portfolio shift in its direction. However, such responses need not reflect more saving but just some other asset's (or its return's) decline. Economy-wide, both econometrics and country experience suggest that the overall saving rate does not react to the rate of interest.[27]

Even if saving propensities shift upward, extra resource flows will not materialize unless there is higher investment demand. Otherwise potential saving surpluses will vent in the form of reduced commodity purchases or speculation. The market may not take advantage of potential saving for well-known reasons. As noted in Section 3.1, many developing countries have evolved mixed economies in which public investment complements private capital formation. Without a programme to expand state projects, overall investment may not grow. In economies where investment has a high import content (say sixty per cent in sub-Saharan Africa), additional foreign resources are needed to complement extra domestic saving, unless economic activity and intermediate imports contract. In import-strangled countries forty per cent of investment becomes an upper bound on saving flows.

Related problems arise with financial intermediation. If savers insist on short-term deposits (under inflation, for example), banks have difficulty in lending long. Publicly backed development banks or corporations dominate the long end of Third World lending—if they don't exist, they are usually invented. With a public investment and intermediation structure in place, saving increases

[26] The theoretical justification for policies for promoting financial 'deepening' or 'derepression' appears in the tracts by Shaw (1973) and McKinnon (1973). Country-level applications are taken up in Sections 4.4 and 4.5.

[27] The literature on this issue is enormous, far too extensive to summarize here. Giovannini (1985) gives the flavour of the debate, and presents regressions coming down soundly against any interest rate effect on national savings rates for Asian countries, where the phenomenon is advertised by financial derepressionists as being strong.

can in principle be directed to productive use. But if this apparatus is not brought into play, raising interest rates is likely to have its usual effect of causing output contraction. Traditionally, tight credit is used to slow down activity when the economy is overheated. It is not obvious why growth should accelerate if the policy is extended into the medium run.

The second interest rate channel involves the possibility that higher rates will not only cause contraction, but also inflation from working capital cost-push, as discussed in Section 3.2. The problem is exacerbated if higher deposit rates in the regulated part of the financial system draw assets from relatively efficient curb markets toward banks where credit multipliers are low. Total financial intermediation shrinks, raising the cost of working capital even more.[28] Financial deregulation may make the situation one step worse, by forcing the replacement of cheap demand deposits in banks by liquid assets bearing high rates (as has occurred over the past decade in the United States). If the new paper is issued by entities besides the commercial banks, the stage is set for disintermediation and a credit crunch. An illuminating example occurred in the Philippines, where high interest rate liabilities issued by the central bank to finance Present Marcos's political manipulations pulled deposits from the commercial banks, forcing loan contraction and output recession.

Third, there may be collapse of credit demand in a recession which is exacerbated by high rates. As firms struggle or fail, banks end up with excess liquidity which cannot be lent. This problem appeared in Ghana, Tanzania, Mexico, Peru, and other countries in the WIDER sample. It is not easily remedied by attempts at credit creation, which boil down to 'pushing on a string', in the traditional phrase. Direct demand stimulation (foreign exchange and other limitations permitting) is required.

The last important interest rate linkage runs through the capital account of the balance of payments. In Section 3.3 we noted that world-market interest rates serve as a reference point for the local rate structure. However, exchange rate policy obviously enters

---

[28] The effect is recognized in several of the WIDER studies, and has been widely discussed in South Korea. See van Wijnbergen (1983) for econometrics on the Korean curb market.

investors' perceptions of returns, and possible financial instabilities arise. These are discussed below.

The next topic is the inflation tax (or seignorage), a reliable perennial in the monetarist gardener's eye. With the recent burst in inflation in developing countries, it is attracting renewed interest among mainstream economists, especially as flashier rational expectations blossoms wither and fade. Structuralists are also beginning to build inflation taxes into their models, although without the monetarists' habitual assumption that output is determined from the side of supply.

To understand how the tax works, it is useful to begin with the equation of exchange (money supply × velocity = price × output) from Section 2.1. In the discussion so far, this relationship has been treated as an asset demand rule upon which monetarist inflation theories can be based. At the same time, macroeconomic adjustment has been analyzed through income–expenditure balances—Keynes's and Kalecki's principle of effective demand.

From the history of the debate over the *General Theory*, one may recall that Pigou and Patinkin proposed a counter-principle now called the 'real balance effect' through which a rise in the price level reduces the real value of the public's stock of money. Citizens' desires to restore lost wealth should lead their saving rates to go up and activity to decline. Similarly, a price decrease following upon wage cuts would stimulate demand and generate employment, negating a central argument of Keynes.[29]

At first the effect was treated as an empirically irrelevant theoretical curiosity, but over the years it gained stature to the point of replacing Keynesian effective demand. In standard contemporary models, macro balance derives from a reshuffled equation of exchange: output demand = money supply × velocity/price. Real aggregate spending becomes *only* an inverse function of the price

---

[29] Keynes argued in Chapter 19 of the *General Theory* that because prices follow from wages through cost functions or mark-ups, money wage reductions just make prices fall proportionately, leaving the real wage and output unchanged. His model presupposes constant effective demand, incorporating the 'principle' mentioned in the text. Pigou and Patinkin wanted to add a restriction—full employment—to Keynes's model closure. To avoid over-determination, they postulated the real balance effect as an adjustment mechanism. Forced saving gives the same result, since it also sets up a negative relationship between the price level and real aggregate demand.

level, a proposition far stronger than the real balance effect (plus the complementary 'Keynes effect' on investment due to lower interest rates resulting from higher real balances). That this reduced form specification elides class differentials in income flows and saving propensities, investment and export functions, and a host of other relationships does not distress orthodox practitioners.

The inflation tax (which itself traces at least to the cumulative process inflation models of Wicksell eighty years ago) translates this story into an analysis of saving-limited growth. The sequence of events is straightforward. A government running a cash deficit covers by borrowing from the central bank. The money supply, via the usual credit multiplier, rises proportionately. From the equation of exchange in its asset demand guise, the price level rises in proportion to that (if economic activity and velocity are assumed constant). What happens to macroeconomic balance as the inflation rate goes up?

If money pays no interest, the instantaneous decrease in the real value of the current stock is given by the rule loss of wealth = inflation rate × money supply. Suppose that rentiers step up their saving precisely to offset their capital loss. Through the printing press, they cede the government a 'tax' equal to the product of the rate of inflation and the money supply. If they learn to hold less money so that velocity rises as inflation accelerates (an empirical truism), the tax base contracts. Monetary theorists like to ponder the shape of the Laffer Curve (relating tax base with tax rate) under such circumstances, but for practical purposes we can leave such conundrums aside. Three more serious considerations arise.

First, if the inflation tax is really paid it should reduce aggregate demand. This problem is usually evaded in monetarist models by the full employment assumption. Increased fiscal spending is exactly offset by more rentiers' saving, so that all that occurs is a transfer from holders of money to the state. However, if capacity use can vary, increasing any tax ought to make output decline. (In this regard, the real balance story makes more sense than the usual inflation tax analysis, since Pigou and Patinkin at least permitted real output to adjust to demand.)

An obvious counter-measure to the demand impact of the tax under structural inflation is to index money, paying an interest rate on state debt equal to the rate of inflation. This interest component of fiscal spending can sky-rocket to ten per cent of nominal GDP with three-digit inflation. Despite the awesome numbers, in principle no net demand injection is involved—monetary indexation just offsets the inflation tax. The reasoning seems clear but was not accepted by IMT teams during failed negotiations over seven Letters of Intent in Brazil. Argentine negotiators also faced the same problem. In mid-1986, however, the IMF agreed not to count monetary indexation against the Public Sector Borrowing Requirement in Mexico. Monetarist rationality does penetrate the Fund.

The second observation is that Fund teams may not have been so unsubtle in their understanding of the effects of inflation on aggregate demand after all. Inflation obviously affects real returns to all forms of wealth, not just money. When arbitrage in the manner of Irving Fisher does not drive real interest rates to equality with real profit rates (or more generally equalize all the economy's rates of return), there can be significant transfer effects. That is why debtors traditionally favour inflation and lenders detest it. On the downside, inflation control can easily ruin balance sheets of debtor firms, leading to what Fisher (1933) called a 'debt-deflation' crisis involving bankruptcies and the firms' inability to use their real capital stock for productive purposes. In this case, slower inflation leads aggregate demand to fall, whereas if inflation taxes are important consumption will rise. Under big changes in the inflation rate, these wealth effects propagate economy-wide and make macro forecasting even more than normally imprecise.

The third point is that the tax is the monetarist distributional angle on inflation, working through shifts in real wealth and rates of saving.[30] The structuralist angle is forced saving, whereby with faster inflation the income distribution shifts against those with incompletely indexed payment flows, and they are driven to spend less in real terms. The two processes are complementary, operate simultaneously, and cannot be disentangled in practice.

As we already noted with regard to money, a 'solution' to both problems is generalized indexation of financial and production-related contracts. Indexation works, to the extent that distributio-

---

[30] We forgo discussing yet another story that says real consumption of durables and real estate rises with the onset or acceleration of inflation, since their prices can be expected to go up along with all the others. The demand injection from consumption will rise and saving rates as measured in the national accounts will fall.

nal conflicts are softened and the incompatible income claims at the root of inflation veiled. But as it becomes entrenched, the inflationary process acquires the inertia discussed in Section 2.1. Any upward price excursion (say a discrete devaluation, a jump in import prices, or an internal shock) feeds through the indexation rules to push inflation to a new plateau. At some point resistance appears. Rational business planning becomes impossible with rapidly and erratically varying prices; social tension may be on the rise.

The bold stroke against inertia is a 'heterodox shock' of the form enacted in the mid-1980s in Argentina, Peru, and Brazil.[31] These programmes resembled previous structuralist stabilizations in embodying a strong element of price control from the side of costs—wage and exchange rate freezes and caps on interest rates—as well as attempts to keep mark-ups in line by price checks, mobilization of public opinion, and moral suasion. They also nullified the indexation of contracts by rewriting them in terms of a new currency unit through elaborate conversion tables, and embodied diverse political commitments to restrain demand and redistribute income as discussed below.

It is too early for a thorough evaluation of these attempts, although by mid-1987 it was fair to say that the Brazilian programme had broken down, while the Argentine rate (after a two-year pause) was again entering double digits. The Peruvian package was primarily oriented towards economic reactivation and redistribution along stagnationist lines, but inflation was not strongly accelerating. These programmes are discussed in more detail in Chapter 4, but some summary conclusions can be offered here.

The key observation is that it is difficult to arrive at an appropriate stance regarding fiscal, monetary, and redistributive policy during the period of the shock since aggregate demand will be changing in response to hard-to-quantify forces—a point neatly put in model form by Ros (1987). As we have just noted, consumption may rise with slower inflation because forced saving and contractionary wealth effects such as the inflation tax are

---

[31] The name was proposed by Lopes (1984), and an English-language presentation of the theory of intertial inflation and monetary reform appears in Arida and Lara-Resende (1985).

undone. On the other hand, demand may fall because the tax collection apparatus functions more effectively in real terms with slower inflation while higher real interest rates retard investment demand. All these factors (plus others) appeared in Brazil and Argentina, but their balance in both cases involved output expansion in a stagnationist macro system.[32]

The programmes' designers did not foresee such strong consumption responses. They were less visible in Argentina where the programme was self-consciously neutral on fiscal and distributional lines than in Brazil where there was an 8 per cent nominal wage increase leading into the shock. In neither country was fiscal programming easy because of inadequate data about the myriad transactions between the central government, local governments, and the public enterprises including defence-related activities. The initial fiscal injection may have been underestimated in Brazil because of this number swamp and the difficulty of gauging how much demand was really being generated by the monetary indexation rules.

The demand surges led immediately to problems in controlling flex-prices; principally those of food products and some services. A sequence of positive price excursions ensued in specific markets in both countries, which were difficult to foresee and offset with stock draw-downs or imports. Indeed, by late 1986 Santos port in Brazil may have been so congested with food coming in that exports could not get out and foreign exchange strangulation at least briefly threatened. Essential prices were still not under control, however, in part because suppliers held back stocks in speculation against further price rises in the near future. They turned out to be right.

With the upward drift in the consumer price index from these events, real incomes eroded and pressures rose for a wage increase. Devaluation was required to offset exchange appreciation. But then through the mark-up mechanism industrial prices (which were fairly effectively controlled after the shocks) went up, and the stage

[32] One destabilizing linkage involved Brazilian automobile firms which had apparently been planning a price increase just before the freeze. When the heterodox shock was decreed, relative car prices were low and demand correspondingly strong. Improved tax collection did show up in Argentina, in an 'effect' well-known since the European hyperinflations of the 1920s. It is analyzed by Olivera (1967) and Tanzi (1977), among many others.

was set for a resurgent price spiral. In Argentina, as noted, an inflationary plateau was held for a time. In Brazil political considerations precluded contractionary fiscal actions for several months after the demand pressures became apparent in mid-1986 (a few months after the shock). But the economic dynamics overrode the timing of events the political leaders had in mind. Financial paper bearing triple-digit annual interest rates began to appear while inflation itself was still only about 2 per cent per month, in anticipation of an automatic wage trigger at 20 per cent accumulated inflation which was set off late in the year. In an economy growing faster than 10 per cent in late 1986, a new inflation was soon underway. Without active intervention (such as a new three-month freeze attempted in June 1987), it may tend towards hyperinflation, as Modiano (1987) shows with hindsight in a formal inertial inflation model that takes interactions between the 8 per cent initial wage increase and the 20 per cent trigger into account.

Two final notes should be added. First, structural inflations spring at base from social conflict (as revealed for example in flex-price movements), a detail that purely inertial models omit. How to balance financial stability, distributional claims, the fiscal and monetary stance, and the transition between stagnationist and forced saving adjustment modes are questions central to any heterodox programme, and their answers can never be very clear, Second, as the low relative Brazilian car prices (footnote 32) illustrate, it is helpful to go into a shock with a price structure consistent with micro-level patterns of supply and demand. There is no sure way to know that prices will be in line, but a 'balanced' inflation with more or less equal rates of growth of prices and components of cost might be a propitious omen.

The 'heterodox' usage was coined in criticism of previous orthodox stabilization attempts in Latin America. These largely took two forms. The first was the 'old' monetarist approach based on fiscal and monetary austerity pure and simple. On the whole, such policies failed to reduce inflation when there was a degree of social resistance on the part of important groups to real income cuts. Tight money in an economy characterized by fix-price rules (either mark-ups or administered prices) and widespread indexation mechanisms just forces a period of recession followed by a new inflationary burst. In practice the output losses were worsened by a persistent tendency on the part of local authorities and the IMF to underestimate inflation rates, as in Brazil in the 1960s, Chile in the 1970s (where understated inflation also showed up in the national accounts, exaggerating reported output growth rates), and Mexico more recently. *Ex post*, with price projections set too low, pre-specified nominal wage payments and fiscal outlays are cut back in real terms, leading to output contraction.

The WIDER countries in which old-fashioned monetarism had some success were characterized by the dominance of flex-price markets (the Philippines and African countries) and/or repressive regimes (Chile, where it took five years of unemployment rates well over 20 per cent for inflation to be driven down from 600 to 30 per cent). In Ghana and Tanzania, inflation abatement was aided by good weather and capital inflows at the right time. Excess commodity demands that were initially caused by poor weather and fed into forced saving were reduced.[33]

'New' monetarism in Latin America took the form of exchange rate manipulations and liberalization aimed at doing away with inflation through reducing expectations and applying the law of one price. As already noted in Section 2.1, these attempts failed, but it is of interest to trace through the financial dislocations they created. That discussion leads into the final topic of this section—the problems implicit in bail-outs of a fragile financial system.

Financial instability showed up in the form of capital movements.[34] Southern Cone economic teams strongly influenced by the rational expectations doctrine tried to attack inflation by reducing the rate of depreciation of the crawling peg (to zero in Chile and in line with a preannounced *tablita* in Argentina).[35] The

[33] Outside the WIDER sample, Bolivia represents a recent monetarist 'success'. However, the abolition of hyperinflation there involved real wage cuts approaching 50 per cent over the first quarter of stabilization and 25 per cent over the first year, widening of the trade deficit as protection was removed, industrial activity decreases approaching 15 per cent, and severe political dislocations. As Morales (1987) and Ocampo (1987b) further note, there were no signs of economic recuperation 18 months after the orthodox shock.

[34] Diaz-Alejandro (1981) ably recounts the history of these stabilizations. Frenkel (1983) works out a formal model which underlies the discussion in the text.

[35] In Argentine patois, this sort of policy embodies an 'active' crawling peg. A more traditional 'passive' crawl just adjusts the exchange rate in line with the difference between the domestic and world inflation rates to hold the real exchange rate stable. The passive version works against (instead of stimulating) destabilizing capital movements of the type described in the text.

policy altered relative returns on domestic and foreign assets. It had fairly complicated general equilibrium effects, which are worth tracing through in detail.

In a simple model, the alternative return for the financial system's liabilities at home (bank deposits, say) can be taken to be the interest rate firms pay for productive credit—wealth-holders can either put money in the bank or lend directly to firms. The relevant return on foreign holdings is the interest rate abroad *plus* the rate of depreciation. An active, slow downward crawl made foreign holdings less attractive. Therefore bank deposits looked better. Purely in terms of asset substitution, the interest rate should have risen when the crawl was slowed, to keep up the attractiveness of loans to firms as rentiers switched assets towards domestic deposits.

However, when the active crawl went into force, capital moved towards the country from abroad. It increased bank reserves since the current account deficit could not widen instantly to absorb the desired inflow. The resulting credit expansion overrode any substitution effects from the lower foreign return, so that in the general equilibrium adjustment, interest rates fell. Southern Cone economies enjoyed a boom, while structural inflation did not slow anywhere near as rapidly as had been planned. Increasing real appreciation finally provoked worries about a future maxi-devaluation to sanitize the current account. With fully liberalized exchange markets, the capital flow reversed. The flight was supported for a couple of years by extensive foreign borrowing as governments attempted to sustain the appreciated exchange rate. The money went out as fast as it came in, adding up to tens of billions of dollars before the debt bubble broke in the wake of the Malvinas/Falklands War in 1981 and the Mexican collapse some months later. Successor economic teams were left to clean up the financial mess.

The histories of capital flight in anticipation of depreciation and associated with a build-up of foreign debt were broadly similar in Argentina, Mexico, and elsewhere. Firms, local banks, and the state were left with large foreign liabilities; citizens held assets abroad. Typically the government and/or central bank had to absorb the private foreign liabilities by allowing firms to exchange them for local currency advances. In effect, a massive rediscount operation was undertaken, whereby the central bank discounted the advances commercial banks made to firms to 'cover' their dollar debt.

Local variants involved large wealth effects. In Mexico, for example, savers who had built up Mex-dóllar deposits (really peso deposits denominated in dollars) were taxed by conversion of their holdings to pesos at an unfavourable rate, although they still reaped capital gains. In Argentina, nearly 100 per cent reserve requirements were imposed on bank deposits to sustain confidence. Any new bank lending, therefore, required immediate rediscount—the central bank became the only financial intermediary in the system. Meanwhile, the high interest rates in the commercial banks' deposits required a continuous infusion of money from the central bank to keep their cash flows positive. A new concept, the 'quasi-fiscal deficit', appeared in Argentine accounts to describe the transfer flow.

In these countries and elsewhere (notably Brazil, where a similar bail-out took place) unlimited rediscounting created political problems. Populist provincial governments, for example, could spend freely and cover their outlays by borrowing from their local development banks. The central bank obligingly rediscounted the provincial bank paper, making the money supply virtually impossible to control. Until the regional politicians were brought into line, the problem was structural in the sense that with a globally fragile financial system the rediscount window could not be closed.

3.5 Other Markets, Black and Grey

Financial difficulties at least have the virtue of being visible. In other situations the workings of macro adjustment are difficult to discern. All economic systems rely to an extent on markets that are illegal or at least not well reflected in the official statistics. Several are important to stabilization.

First, with exchange controls in effect there will be a parallel exchange rate. In some countries, it mediates transactions that are truly 'black'. Elsewhere there is a tolerated unofficial market or perhaps legal dual or multiple rates. Capital flows, tourism, and/or non-traditional exports typically transact at a depreciated rate; appreciated rates apply to essential imports or mono-exports so that they trade with low cost or remuneration in local currency terms. In some countries, such as Egypt and the Sudan, multiple rates are an honoured way of life, and shifting commodities between categories is one way of doing a real devaluation.

In practical stabilizations, a variable dual rate is often used as an indicator of confidence in the programme. Local financial markets operate with benchmark levels for the premium of the parallel over the official rate: say from a few percentage points negative in Colombia from time to time (apparently because of drug dealers who want to trade in their dollars) to plus fifty in many corners of the world. When the premium gets too high, policy-makers fear capital flight and destabilizing speculation. The high premium may feed back positively into these processes via expectations, or else cut them off. Either way, it is a signal of financial distress.

One can view the parallel exchange market, the internal financial market, and macro balance as a three-dimensional flex-price/fix-price system with the parallel exchange rate, the interest rate, and output as adjusting variables. On the basis of several schemes for forming expectations, Kamin (1987) argues that depreciation of the official rate may make the dual rate devalue, at times more than proportionately.[36] In so far as it influences actual trade flows, the parallel rate may transmit contractionary effects of devaluation more directly than its official twin. The interactions in this three-way system wrap around themselves intricately, but the success of a stabilization attempt may depend on partially untying the knot. Trying to cut it with a market knife such as a foreign exchange auction usually fails, though such schemes recur over time. They are fashionable in orthodox African stabilizations at the moment, but court destabilizing speculation and seem to bias the import bill toward consumer goods. See Section 4.1.

Within the domestic economy, parallel markets for commodities can also spread, especially when the state's price and quantity controls lose their edge. The unofficial markets range from being a minor headache to the policy team to a symptom of political disintegration. The 'black economy' and tax evasion are widely discussed in India. Widespread parallel transactions represent a major problem for stabilization in Tanzania, Ghana, Nicaragua, and elsewhere—their prices rise reflecting forced saving, and feed back into inflation throughout the system. Corruption goes hand-

---

[36] Attempts at 'wiping out speculators' by maxi-devaluation are likely to fail if the premium goes up. Such an occurrence contributed to the fall of an Egyptian finance minister some years ago. Official grower price increases in Tanzania in 1984 had a similar effect, driving up informal prices more than in proportion.

in-hand with these shadow markets all over the world. When the economy is tightly foreign-exchange and food constrained, the rules for transactions presupposed by most neoclassical and Marxist economists are subsumed into broader games involving carving out space in urban subsistence activities and contestable rights to access to the resources of the countryside. Neither orthodox nor heterodox stabilization policies have much to do with such phenomena. Indeed, from a market-oriented perspective, liberalization is not likely to bring efficiency gains when parallel markets are common, since their prices are already uncontrolled.

In brief, parallel markets may be only the tip of a social and economic iceberg; there is virtually no information about what it looks like below the waterline. The iceberg may melt as stabilization takes hold. Indeed, one might think that the non-indexed, flex-price nature of parallel markets may make monetarist anti-inflation programmes relatively effective. However, that ignores the oligopolistic structures they often develop. The only effective means for blasting away at these entrenched positions are large increases in supply or massive demand contraction. What rapid expansion of parallel transactions does signal is a breakdown of the modern economy (including the ability of the government to maintain its revenue base) that may be difficult to restore. Manufacturing and other relatively sophisticated processes seem to operate best in a fix-price environment. One goal of stabilization should be to build such a framework back up after it has been damaged by the transformation of fix- to flex-prices under external strangulation or binding output constraints.

3.6 A Checklist of Stabilizations

To a large extent, macroeconomic theory amounts to a catalogue of 'effects', some in mode at a tiven time, some empirically relevant, some with a basis in theory. Chapters 2 and 3 have presented the effects emphasized in the WIDER studies. Not all are fashionable, but they do apply in developing country contexts.

By way of review, the major linkages are set out in Table 1, in the form of a checklist which future designers of stabilization policy might want to bear in mind. The entries overlap to an extent, on the principle that redundancy is preferable to omitting important items.

The first section of the table lists the elements of the policy background—the nature of macro shocks, the configuration of the social matrix, and other initial conditions. The second section summarizes the factors influencing overall macro behaviour of the economy, which determine how an appropriate model might be 'closed'. The third section points to specific macro linkages that were emphasized in the WIDER papers and no doubt show up elsewhere in the Third World. The final section lists possible effects of different policy moves that it makes sense to take into account.

The main purpose of the table is to summarize the discussion so far and underline the questions that the WIDER studies have posed. In broad form, it also suggests categories for the stabilization episodes that the countries went through, as we will see in the following chapter.

Table 1 Checklist of Factors Relevant for Policy Design

I. Background: nature of shocks requiring stabilization, the social matrix, and other considerations.

A. External shocks
   i. External strangulation (causes could include adverse shifts in the terms of trade, falling export volume, falling remittance and/or capital inflows, higher interest rate on debt, etc.)
   ii. Foreign exchange bonanza (What are the causes? How long will they last?)

B. Internal shocks
   i. Inflation (structuralist or monetarist causes?)
   ii. Internal financial crisis (What are asset and liability positions of involved groups?)
   iii. Capital flight by nationals (What are links to internal finance and external considerations?)
   iv. Past policy errors (examples include over-expansion, infeasible attempts at income redistribution, a badly over-valued exchange rate, etc.)
   v. Natural and man-made shocks (harvest failures, other natural disasters, war).

C. Other external considerations
   i. Is the real exchange rate badly over-valued?
   ii. Will stabilization draw in official assistance or permit access to international capital markets? If so, how soon? Will inflows only respond to orthodoxy, or to better performance overall?

D. Social matrix and political considerations
    i. What are major groups in the social matrix?
    ii. What are the production flows and key prices associated with each group?
    iii. What are each group's major assets and liabilities, and how are their rates of return and prices determined?
    iv. What are the political roles of the major groups?
    v. What policy options are available to help the poor and vulnerable population groups?
    vi. Other political considerations—geopolitics, regime stability and compromises, etc.

II. Overall macroeconomic linkages and structure
A. Output adjustment
    i. Is output free to vary upward and downward within some range?
    ii. If so, how wide is the range? Is macro response stagnationist (progressive income redistribution stimulates demand) or exhilarationist (regressive redistribution stimulates demand or perhaps output via substitution responses)?
    iii. If output is fixed, what is (are) the limiting factor(s); e.g. foreign resources, overall capacity, sectoral capacities, infrastructure?
    iv. With output fixed, what are major channels for macro adjustment via forced saving or the inflation tax?
B. Process of inflation
    i. What are structural elements in inflation, i.e. distributional conflicts and propagation mechanisms such as contract indexation?
    ii. Are monetary or excess demand factors important? If so, how do price increases caused by demand factors map into increases of components of cost?
C. Sectoral disaggregations
    i. Are there relevant disaggregations, such as agriculture *vs.* non-agriculture, traded *vs.* non-traded, etc?
    ii. If so, what are adjustment mechanisms by sector, e.g. flex-price with output fixed or in inelastic supply, fix-price with output (or net trade) adjusting, or something else?
D. Balance of payments considerations
    i. How effective are exchange controls? Do they permit some degree of freedom in determining internal interest rates?
    ii. Are remittance flows important? If so, what are mechanisms that can be used to control or capture part of the flow?
    iii. Are debt obligations important? Is debt mostly external and state-

owned? If so, how is the double transfer problem (national resources to the state plus a trade surplus) to be orchestrated?

    iv. More drastically, is partial repudiation of external payment obligations for debt on the cards?

E. Financial market considerations

    i. Has there been (or will there have to be) a bail-out of firms or banks with balance-sheet problems? What were (or will be) the effects on net wealth positions and returns?

    ii. What are elements of fragility in the system, and particular problems in its management?

III. Special macroeconomic linkages

A. Does public investment crowd in or crowd out private investment? What are the channels and how can they be affected by policy?

B. Will a shift in the terms of trade toward agriculture stimulate or retard demand for non-agricultural goods? Are there intra-sectoral distributional and/or supply conflicts, for example between food and export agriculture?

C. Are levels of demand likely to be influenced by wealth effects?

    i. Changes in the inflation tax due to stabilization and/or modification of indexation of components of the money supply and contracts more generally.

    ii. Changes in balance sheet positions of debtors and creditors when the inflation rate shifts markedly.

    iii. Changes in net wealth positions at home and abroad following a maxi-devaluation.

D. Will the efficiency of the tax collection apparatus be affected by shifts in the inflation rate and/or policy manoeuvres? Will indirect tax rate increases drive up inflation from the side of costs?

E. Is the economy externally constrained? If so, what are import contents of domestic production and capital formation, and how are trade-offs between output and investment or food and export agriculture to be managed? Will devaluation be expansionary under the circumstances?

F. Will exports increase if domestic absorption is restrained? How lagged will the response be?

G. Factors influencing inflation

    i. Is the overall price level influenced by foreign prices, completely or partially? What about sectoral prices?

    ii. What is the relative importance of fix- and flex-price markets? Have fix-price rules become increasingly flex under supply constraints? What is the role of the traders' margins in flex-price markets?

    iii. How widespread are indexation rules for wages, the exchange rate, commodity prices, bank deposits, financial contracts, etc?

    iv. Will interest rate increases or credit restrictions feed into inflation by increasing the cost of financing working capital?

    v. Will indirect tax-rate increases be inflationary?

H. Other interest rate effects

    i. Will interest rate increases lead to more private saving? If so, how can it be absorbed macroeconomically?

    ii. What shifts in portfolios will changes in interest rates induce? How will they affect overall intermediation of the financial system?

    iii. Under recession, will high rates choke off credit demand so effectively that the banking system ends up with excess liquidity?

    iv. What will be the effect of high rates on fiscal cash-flow—will they be applied fully to state obligations? If so, does a serious financing problem arise? What will be the macro effects of the reduction in government saving, if it is real (i.e. not just due to indexation of public liabilities)?

I. Is there potential excess saving in the economy for any reason? Aside from holding output down, is it likely to be diverted into capital flight and/or domestic speculation in real estate, shares, etc? Is there any danger of Ponzi schemes or a bubble in newly deregulated or inadequately regulated financial markets?

J. Is there a parallel exchange rate under capital controls? Is destabilizing exchange speculation or capital flight likely in anticipation of a maxi-devaluation?

K. Are there macroeconomically important public sector agencies, e.g. export marketing boards, food subsidy agencies, etc? How should they fit into a stabilization programme.

IV. Special policy questions

A. Devaluation

    i. Is it inflationary? If not, what are reasons (e.g. wiping out quota rents, etc)?

    ii. Is it contractionary? If so, for how long before J-curve responses become important? What are factors underlying contractionary response, e.g. real wage effects, initial trade deficit, the role of export marketing boards?

    iii. Is it expansionary? If so, from quota rents, a binding foreign exchange constraint, export response, or what?

    iv. Will changes in the rate of a crawling peg influence relative returns of foreign and domestic assets enough to induce major capital movements?

B. Effects of trade liberalization

    i. Will liberalization lead to jumps in imports of consumer (or other specific classes) of goods?

    ii. Is de-industrialization in response to liberalization likely?

    iii. What will be the effects on price formation generally and by sectors?

    iv. Will liberalization (or possibly raising trade barriers to guarantee local markets) call forth capital inflows and/or direct foreign investment?

C. Effects of an import quota regime

    i. Are quota changes expansionary or contractionary?

    ii. Do quotas forestall inflation when there is devaluation?

D. Balance of payments responses

    i. Can quotas, subsidies, and other policies be efficiently directed to stimulate exports or import substitution? If so, in what time frame?

    ii. What is the role of public investment in improving 'tradability' economy-wide or by sector?

    iii. What is the role of incomes policies, e.g. in reducing absorption to stimulate exports?

    iv. What are specific policies to affect remittance flows and control capital movements?

    v. Does a foreign exchange auction make sense? Can it be set up to avoid bias in favour of imports of consumer goods and dangers of speculation?

E. Publicly controlled prices

    i. Will increases of public enterprise prices be inflationary via cost-push or deflationary by reducing the public sector deficit and money emission? Which effect is stronger?

    ii. Distributional and aggregate demand effects of changes in publicly controlled prices, e.g. food subsidies and farmgate prices as regulated by marketing boards.

F. Are conditions favourable for a heterodox anti-inflation shock?

    i. 'Balanced' inflation rate, i.e. more or less equal rates of increase of major components of cost and elements in the price index.

    ii. Widespread, formalized indexation.

    iii. What are the fiscal and distributional dimensions of the shock package? What will be their effects on aggregate demand, and risks of provoking forced saving via a consumption surge?

G. Incomes policies and human welfare

    i. How do incomes policies fit into the linkages in the social matrix?

    ii. Under stagnationist adjustment, what is the room for progressive redistribution before output limits will begin to bind?

    iii. If forced saving adjustment processes are important, what relative price changes and social groups are involved? Will attempts at redistribution by price policy (such as food subsidies) malfunction due to supply constraints?

iv. If inflation responds to demand factors or money emission, how do price changes map into mechanisms for generation of income by social and economic class?

v. Can stabilization be oriented to help the poor and vulnerable population groups, i.e. can it have a 'human face'?

H. The bottom line: is a proposed stabilization package internally consistent and coherent? Will it satisfy internal and external constraints on the economy? In what areas can one expect it to be successful? Where do the main dangers of failure lie?

4

Country Experiences

So far, the discussion shows that stabilizations are triggered by diverse combinations of forces and unfold in distinct environments in space and time. Grouping country experiences in at least three dimensions is tempting, based on the nature of the economic shocks involved, the causal structure or closure of the national economic system, and the types of policies employed. With several categories in each class (internal *vs.* external shocks by type, output or forced saving adjustments by sector, orthodox or heterodox policies of various stripes), a full taxonomy would make the shade of Linnaeus perk up.

Having only 18 countries in the WIDER sample, we cannot pursue the classification game too far. In this chapter, countries are discussed in five categories, based largely on macro shocks and policy responses, with an analysis of closure entering into the discussion of each economy's course. The groups are:

1. Externally strangled small primary product (or labour) exporters: Ghana, Ivory Coast, Kenya, Nicaragua, Sudan, and Tanzania;
2. Countries that encountered foreign bonanzas of varying strength and duration: Colombia, Egypt, Mexico, and the Philippines;
3. Countries where there were fairly orthodox stabilizations with a dose of regressive income redistribution and some balance of payments success: Chile, Sri Lanka, and Turkey;
4. Economies in which heterodox anti-inflationary shocks with progressive redistribution were attempted: Argentina, Brazil, and Peru;
5. Two special cases, one closed and one open to trade: India and South Korea.

Each country's history of stabilization is outlined in the following sections based on this categorization, with emphasis on how its macro system works, the types of shocks it went through, the policy responses, and how policy might have been done better. In most cases, illustrative figures and tables taken from the country papers are used to aid the discussion. Section 4.6 gives a cross-country summary of the results.

4.1 Externally Strangled, Small, Open Economies

The six countries in this group share common problems of economic openness.[1] They export agricultural commodities (or labour directly) in unstable markets with prices that have been on a downtrend since the mid-1970s. All have undergone a degree of import-substituting industrialization; hence, domestic activity requires imported intermediate inputs. With stagnant export revenues, all are foreign-exchange constrained. In several of the countries food-supply lags as well, due to bad weather, slow or negative productivity growth, and rapid population expansion. The food and foreign-exchange constraints interact. If policies are directed toward stimulation of agro-exports, food production may drop off. The resulting inflationary pressures make real appreciation likely. Meanwhile, attempts to direct dollars toward investment in exports will constrain agricultural output because capacity to import fertilizers, fuel, and chemicals will be reduced.

The financial side of small, open economies is typically under-developed—domestic capital seeks safe havens abroad and does not require much internal intermediation. The 'official' part of the market is made up almost exclusively of banks. One implication is that aside from loans from abroad the state cannot place its obligations outside the banking system—fiscal and monetary policy amount to virtually the same thing. Unofficial markets, however, may flourish, especially for food products internally and for dollars or the importables they buy.

With output doubly limited by foreign exchange and conditions of agricultural supply, two broad mechanisms of macro adjustment

[1] Other WIDER countries more or less in the same boat include Colombia and the Philippines (Section 4.2) and Sri Lanka and Chile (Section 4.3). Their cases are discussed later since their stabilization histories involve dealing with a series of bonanzas (Colombia and the Philippines) and consciously regressive income redistributions (the other two).

are possible. The first, characteristic of traditional agro-exporters like Nicaragua under the Somoza regime or the Ivory Coast, involves active state intervention to limit demand to available supply by fiscal and monetary means. Some group seems ordained to lose its jobs when there is an adverse supply shock; for example *campesinos* on the agricultural estates under the Somozas or expatriate African urban workers (mainly in construction) in the Ivory Coast.

The other mode of adjustment is by inflation taxes and forced saving when the state does not (or cannot) manage its demand injections in counter-cyclical fashion. Transformation of fix-price rules into flex, expansion of parallel markets, and proliferation of subsistence modes of production characterize this process as it settles in. These developments appear in Nicaragua under the Sandinista government and to a varying extent over all sub-Saharan Africa. Orthodox monetary restraint superficially seems ideal for inflation stabilization under such circumstances, but the country papers suggest that there are structural factors rendering its success less than complete. Growth, meanwhile, stagnates under food and foreign exchange constraints.

Nicaragua, the only non-African country covered in this section, is of interest since it has gone through a shift between the two macro closures or adjustment regimes. An illuminating preliminary question, according to Bill Gibson (1986), is whether or not adjustment by unemployment as under the Somozas could have persisted. He thinks not. As illustrated in Figure 1, Nicaragua had 5.5 per cent real GDP growth for two decades as capital-intensive production of cotton and beef for export extended over the major part of the fertile Pacific coast region and industry expanded (for a time) to meet demand from the Central American Common Market. But the counterpart was increasing poverty for a growing population caught up in urban marginal activities and subsistence agriculture which stagnated under a cheap food policy and lack of public investment. Worsening wealth and income distributions plus the legendary brutality of the Somoza 'kleptocracy' (Vilas 1984) made the victory in 1979 of the *Frente Sandinista* almost inevitable.

The Sandinista state began by pursuing income and wealth redistribution (including agrarian reform), social investment, and

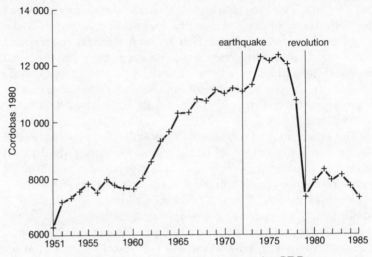

Fig. 1   Nicaragua: Trends in per capita GDP.

fairly strict controls over trade and capital movements. Its initial conditions were not unfavourable. Figure 1 shows how the war itself, a major earthquake in Managua in 1972, and 100-year floods in 1982 damaged or destroyed billions of dollars' worth of capital in an economy where total GDP is only about $3 billion. But on the other hand, foreign loans and transfers to the order of $500 million per year permitted internal and external balance to be maintained with modest growth until 1983. Then came the *contra* counter-revolution causing estimated damages of another $1.5 billion and (in model simulations) a loss of perhaps ten per cent of GDP.

Against this background, Sandinista stabilization policy went through three acts. During the first, from July 1979 through to December 1981, variable prices of non-traded goods replaced fiscal adjustment as the means to attain internal balance. External balance was controlled by regulations over imports and capital movements. Commercial credit was the main monetary instrument with private foreign exchange holdings (going through the black market) adjusting to give portfolio balance. Money supply growth was held to 29 and 24 per cent in 1980 and 1981 respectively, as capital inflows helped cover the fiscal deficit. These changes were premeditated, but it is also true that the growing *contra* threat made the old fiscal mode of adjustment increasingly impractical, as was soon to become clear.

In the second phase, from December 1981 through to October 1983, the invasion expanded and capital inflows dropped off. Inflation began to accelerate as shortages spread, and private investment was crowded out. Measures aimed at changing demand composition to reduce imports did not get very far, and the government went back towards fiscal restraint. The options were to reduce public investment or defence spending; the Sandinistas cut capital formation. Events after 1983 marked a continuation of these trends, as under inflation the state took to the printing press to finance its expanding deficits.

Was there a set of policies available to counteract the degree of strangulation the economy facted in 1986? The labour force had shifted towards parallel market activities in the urban informal sector, as rent-seeking flourished with scarce commodities and dollars. Despite price policies tilted in its favour, export agriculture had begun to confront labour supply problems as Nicaraguans left the countryside for the city (or the army) and migrant workers from neighbouring countries no longer arrived. There had been strong pressure on the black market exchange rate, not alleviated by semi-legal exchange houses and gimmicky auctions of commodities in demand. The latest moves have been towards further austerity, devaluation, and attempts at control over wage increases. In so far as the economy is locked into adjustment via forced saving to meet the war effort, these seem doomed to fail.

If the state withstands the *contra* attack, further problems remain for the future. Closed exchange markets mean that a vehicle for national saving beyond bank accounts must emerge or be created. Indexed saving accounts, Nica-dollars, and similar options suggest themselves, but it is not clear that the national bourgeoisie retains sufficient faith in Sandinista bank inspectors to put its wealth in such accounts. The agricultural labour shortage problem may be addressed by the support of small and medium producers through technical support, credit, and marketing assistance—getting producer prices right has not brought much of an output response from traditional cultivators. Finally, financing the war for a few more quarters by cutting accumulation cannot be a long-term solution. Foreign credits may be available from the Soviet bloc, but then difficult choices will arise about balancing trade and financial flows between the East and partners closer to home.[2]

The Ivory Coast enjoyed a growth rate of more than 7 per cent before the first oil shock. Thereafter the rate declined to 4 per cent until the end of the 1970s. Throughout the two decades before 1980 there were expanding exports of cocoa and coffee, the country's two main crops, and progressive industrialization. The commodity price boom of 1976–77 stimulated public investment which could not be continued when prices dropped off late in the decade. As illustrated in Table 2, the Ivory Coast went through stabilization exercises in 1980–83 and again in 1984.

According to Jacques Pegatienan Hiey (1987), the Ivory Coast government smooths fluctuating export revenues with counter-cyclical policy rules. CAISSTAB, the marketing board, passes more than 50 per cent of export proceeds to producers but shields their income flows in downswings and reaps the surplus when world prices are high. These profits are handed to the government for public investment, so that both revenues and expenditures of the state vary in line with foreign sales.

Since the Ivory Coast is a member of the West African Monetary Union, its exchange rate is pegged to the French franc. It has an open capital market, and has traditionally had good access to foreign loans. The state runs a current fiscal surplus, so both capital inflows and CAISSTAB profits support public investment. The interest rate is pegged, credit is not limited, and saving rises with the level of economic activity: the implication is that state spending crowds private capital formation in. During downswings, construction and urban economic activities contract, since farmers are protected. Although some European expatriate managers were sent packing in the early 1980s, this social group largely has its income flow of about 20 per cent of GDP assured. Non-Ivorian African migrants absorb macroeconomic shocks by losing urban jobs and absorbing wage cuts in rural areas.

Under a conservative, agrarian-oriented government, this traditional quantity-adjusting agro-export model functioned well for

[2] Two options present themselves; full links with the socialist countries along Cuban lines or tripartite arrangements like Angola's. The former is costly in terms of transport and market access, and the other may require a highly marketable export commodity such as oil.

Table 2 Ivory Coast: macroeconomic and balance of payments data
A: Real income—absorption balance

	1979	1980	1981	1982	1983	1984
A. Annual growth rate						
GDP	−3.4	2.25	−5.7	−2.3	0.098	3.2
Disposable income	−0.35	2.11	−5.79	−3.22	0.50	4.94
Consumption						
Private	3.68	3.70	3.27	−4.15	−1.92	1.9
Public	3.4	3.9	−14.4	1.9	−2.6	8.9
Investment						
Private	6.41	−15.28	−30.01	17.78	−20.90	−41.18
Public	−17.5	16.9	9.7	−28.0	−24.8	−43.7
Private saving	−17.3	−1.7	−28.6	0.18	8.9	14.5
Absorption	2.2	3.5	−1.1	−2.7	−6.0	−10.2
Agricultural surplus	−8.3	−25.5	−56.7	67.7	−19.1	182.3
Total public expenditure	−1.74	11.88	2.48	−5.50	−7.94	−22.13
Total public income	−6.19	−5.83	−15.68	10.28	−4.65	22.93
B. Share in GDP (%)						
Private excess saving over investment	7.7	9.7	7.5	5.9	10.1	16.6
Public current savings	−0.96	−1.1	1.0	1.1	1.3	−14.4
Excess absorption	12.0	13.4	18.9	18.4	11.1	−3.3
Fiscal deficit	12.4	17.7	23.5	19.5	17.2	19.5
Agricultural surplus	7.3	5.3	2.4	4.2	3.4	9.3

two decades. However, with price declines and reduced access to foreign credits in 1980, the Ivory Coast was forced to go to the Fund. The main policy applied in a 1981–83 Extended Fund Facility (EFF) was to freeze public investment at its 1980 level in real terms. Slow to negative growth ensued and the current account did not improve. Voluntary capital inflow dropped substantially,

Table 2—*continued*

B: Balance of payments (billions of constant CFA Francs (1980))

	1979	1980	1981	1982	1983	1984
Exports	579.0	656.6	745.0	802.4	787.4	1156.0
Imports	474.9	549.9	563.0	603.3	623.1	587.0
Trade balance	104.1	106.7	182.0	199.0	164.3	569.0
Net transfers	−121.6	−150.4	−147.6	−146.3	−133.0	−129.2
Net services	−276.5	−316.2	−362.0	−408.1	−437.8	−460.0
Current account balance	−294.0	−359.9	−327.6	−355.4	−406.5	−20.2
Net capital flows	240.8	203.0	173.6	305.5	206.7	139.0
Errors and omissions	−16.8	−35.9	0.06	0	0	0
Overall balance	−70.0	−192.8	−154.6	−49.8	−199.8	118.8
Total reserves	31.3	4.2	4.8	0.7	3.6	2.4
Share in GDP (%)						
Trade balance	5.35	4.8	7.83	7.98	6.19	19.83
Current account balance	−15.12	−16.20	−14.1	−14.25	−15.32	−0.70
Net capital flows	12.38	9.13	7.44	12.26	7.79	4.84
Overall balance	−3.6	−8.68	−6.65	−1.99	−7.53	4.14
Debt service	6.52	7.89	10.69	12.89	13.0	9.63
Debt service/ exports	21.91	26.72	33.34	40.04	43.8	23.90
Net debt service/ exports	16.51	26.08	32.69	39.95	43.35	23.69

just when a 'well-behaved' economy needed it most. A follow-up standby agreement in 1984 was associated with short-run recovery. However, higher export prices and better rainfall raise the question as to whether the 1984 package was 'successful' or just not needed at all.

Could additional policies be deployed the next time there is an export shock? Linkages that show up in Ivory Coast models include the crowding-in of private investment by public capital formation, strong cost-push from interest rate increases, sensitivity of imports to bureaucratic restriction, and the CAISSTAB/public investment tie. One should also bear in mind that devaluation for African franc zone economies is not thinkable, but that directed commercial policy interventions may be.

In model simulations, these relationships make fiscal policies aimed at reducing absorption stagflationary. A combination of import quotas and interest rate reductions with cuts in absorption should give better results under adverse shocks. As in many of the country studies, the implicit recommendation is that locally relevant policy initiatives should be combined with sensible austerity to avoid overkilling the economy when there is a threat of external strangulation.

Kenya is a third agro-exporting economy that has traditionally followed prudent policy lines. It differs from the Ivory Coast and Nicaragua, however, in that all its land suitable for crops under ruling technologies has been brought into cultivation. Agricultural expansion in the future will require more intensive techniques (and perhaps the expansion of cultivation into sub-marginal zones), while industrial growth will have to take place under import restrictions. Table 3 presents the major trends.

Stabilization has taken place without full adjustment to these problems, in the view of Rolph van der Hoeven and Jan Vandemoortele (1986). Kenya got early access to official support against external shocks—an EFF with the Fund in 1975 and a structural adjustment loan (SAL) from the World Bank in 1980. Both broke down when government borrowing from the central bank exceeded performance requirements. Conditionality in a 1983 standby with the Fund was satisfied, but by then export prices had turned up mildly, drought was receding, and the Treasury found it easier to deal with the predictable IMF line. The Bank wanted detailed loan covenants which directly influenced growth policy and had implications for the future which were by no means clear. It was less cordially received.

The fact that the EFF and SAL broke down suggests that old-fashioned adjustment to external shocks via austerity, pure and

Table 3   Kenya: GDP growth by sectors and saving–investment balances

A: Real annual growth of GDP in selected sectors of the economy, 1979–80 to 1984–85

Sector	% GDP 1984	Real GDP growth rates					
		1979–1980	1980–1981	1981–1982	1982–1983	1983–1984	1984–1985
Traditional economy	(6.2)	3.6	3.5	3.3	3.6	3.3	4.0
Agriculture	(29.7)	−1.3	6.2	4.6	4.2	−3.7	3.5
Manufacturing	(12.6)	5.7	5.0	2.3	4.5	4.3	4.5
Construction	(4.1)	6.4	8.2	−11.8	−8.8	−6.8	1.1
Trade, hotels, and restaurants	(11.5)	3.5	0.7	−7.2	2.8	4.0	8.1
Government services	(14.5)	5.6	5.3	3.8	4.2	2.9	4.5
Total economy		3.3	5.5	1.8	3.5	0.9	4.1
GDP per capita		−0.4	1.7	−2.1	−0.7	−3.1	0.2

B: Savings and investment balance, 1979–85 (K£ million at current prices)

Year	Private sector savings (a)	Private sector GCF (b)	Public sector GCF (c)	Public savings (d)	Public deficit (e)	Net borrowing from abroad (f)	Grants (g)
1979	108.29	267.51	248.74	214.26	34.48	178.30	15.40
1980	197.78	507.64	281.56	240.82	40.74	328.70	21.90
1981	314.38	536.35	322.46	196.83	125.63	326.90	20.70
1982	394.51	463.68	300.85	83.94	216.91	260.50	25.50
1983	337.50	536.19	274.16	324.31	−50.15	88.89	59.80
1984	416.10	565.60	363.34	306.05	57.29	128.26	78.53
1985	320.04	527.74	354.83	298.16	56.67	179.79	84.58

Private sector savings: $a = b + e - f - g$.
Public deficit: $e = d - c$.

simple, was not politically feasible in Kenya. On the other hand, rapid inflation and forced saving adjustment processes were avoided even though the public deficit went well over ten per cent of GDP in the early 1980s. What were the factors underlying this qualified success?

One element was wage-cutting by incomplete indexation. Real wages fell by 20 per cent over the 1980s, holding inflation to around ten per cent per year. This 'incomes' policy enforced by the state replaced market-driven forced saving, but obviously required a social and political system which could absorb wage cuts of such magnitude. More constructively, the Kenyan economy reduced its ratios of imports to GDP (for intermediates, capital goods, and consumption) by one or two per cent per year over the 1980s with an effective control regime. This restraint programme together with slow growth kept the external wolves at bay.

Strictly orthodox policies with regard to the balance of payments were not successful. Devaluation and incomes policies favouring the agro-export sector produced no supply response. As Table 3 shows, real capital inflows to a market-oriented economy dropped by more than 50 per cent after the debt crisis broke in 1981–82. Within the country, forced saving perhaps began to show up in rising incremental capital–output ratios and profit margins in non-traded sectors (especially construction), but it did not take over the system. Increased real interest rates helped hold down the level of activity, without strong inflationary effects.

In future, simultaneously stimulating export agriculture and food production may prove difficult, given the non-effectiveness of price policies so far and the land constraint. At the same time, aggregate demand may be stagnant because of the regressive changes in the income distribution that have already occurred. Agrarian reform and intelligent policies to support small-scale enterprises may help productivity growth, but forced saving adjustment modes will be an ever-present danger unless the external situation improves. How the successful import restraint programme might be the basis for renewed expansion is by no means clear, but the question is worth exploring. The restraint programme was successful, but also may become self-limiting in that imports can only be cut so far.

Tanzania, Kenya's neighbour, went much further in the direction of inflationary adjustment to external strangulation. The war against Idi Amin combined with declining terms of trade to create foreign exchange shortages at the turn of the present decade. The agricultural price structure had shifted in the direction of food, so that export volume was stagnant. Contractionary policy was pursued, but the 1979–80 and 1980–81 budgets underestimated war costs (largely external) already incurred. Finance from the Bretton Woods agencies and a Donors' Conference (which never materialized) was expected. These capital inflows did not arrive, and the foreign constraint began to bind. Excess aggregate demand was cut back by forced saving, as inflation accelerated 15 points to the 25–35 per cent annual range. Foreign payment arrears were run up, parallel markets spread, and state control over the economy in a socialist oriented system weakened. With the benefit of hindsight one can argue that policy in the early 1980s was insufficiently austere, but the calculation looked more favourable at the time.

Benno Ndulu (1987) describes several attempts at stabilization which followed, in the context of an elaborate debate among Tanzanians and with their foreign donors about the directions the economy should take. Partly because discussion had to precede action, programmes came in late and lurching fashion and produced indifferent results (see Table 4). The exchange rate was an especially controversial issue. A Fund request for a 60 per cent maxi-devaluation in 1979 provoked internal resistance, because influential academics and policy-makers had the short-run adverse effects (recounted in Section 3.2) firmly in mind. The outcome was a series of late and jumpy depreciations instead of a managed crawl which might have emerged had Fund pressure not led to local counter-pressure. Similar problems arose with the degree of austerity to be imposed. Working agreement among the Tanzanian government, the World Bank, the Donors' Group, and the Fund was not really attained until 1985–86.

Capital inflows in the first part of the 1980s were about half of the amounts projected in the stabilization programmes: absence of support from the World Bank was notable. The dollars that did arrive were not very effectively utilized since they were tied to investment projects and could not be spent to bring in intermediate imports to support production or to maintain existing capital stock.

While all the negotiation was going on, the economy proved difficult to manage. Internal pricing policy is one example. Losses resulting from attempts by the parastatal marketing boards to support internal prices for export crops led to reductions in enterprise capital formation. The domestic crop board struggled with arrears run up in 1977–80. These deficits ultimately were passed to the government. No real resource cost was involved in this refinancing, *pace* the IMF which argued that there would be inflationary consequences, but it still engendered controversy.

Table 4 Tanzania: Major economic indicators

	1976	1977	1978	1979	1980	1981	1982	1983	1984
Real GDP growth rate (%)		2.8	2.9	1.2	0.8	−1.1	1.3	−0.4	2.5
Per capital GDP growth rate (%)		−0.5	−0.4	−2.1	−2.5	−4.4	−2.0	−3.7	−0.8
Inflation rate (%)	6.9	11.6	13.2	13.0	30.2	25.6	28.9	27.1	36.0
Balance of trade deficit (Shs. million)	1242	1697	5127	4589	6142	4747	6572	5905	76240

The annual inflation rate remained around 30 per cent in the first part of the 1980s; there were high premiums on importables. The rents associated with the import trade and the parallel markets were one symptom of adjustment through forced saving. Others included the expansion of urban subsistence activites and work-sharing. Output was stagnant despite an overall fiscal deficit approaching 15 per cent of GDP (8 or 9 per cent owed abroad, and 3 per cent to the domestic banking system). Banks had excess liquidity—private credit demand was flat in an exchange-bound economy.

The major stabilization effort came in July 1984: there was devaluation, price subsidies and controls were abolished, imports were liberalized, and price incentives were rigged in favour of food-producing agriculture. Inflation immediately accelerated to 45 per cent per year. It then slowed to 25 per cent in 1985 as wages and official food prices were not raised at all. The latter move amounted to a *de facto* restoration of food subsidies to hold down the cost of living, and was assisted by a food supply increase in 1985 and thereafter. Import liberalization apparently played some role in reducing consumer product inflation, as more legal imports of such commodities (but not intermediate or capital goods) came in. Export supply did not increase. In 1985 attempts to raise export crop prices without further devaluation drove the export parastatals back into the red.

On the basis of this experience, Ndulu suggests that future stabilization efforts should include significant external resource mobilization, a maxi-devaluation linked with income tax reductions and increases in wages at the low end of the scale,[3] institution of a crawling peg after the maxi to hold the real exchange rate constant, an aggregate demand policy consistent with foreign constraints, and institutional changes and public investment so that price policies aimed at stimulating exports can actually have some effect. On the fiscal side, a restoration of growth should lead towards balance as both the sales tax and company tax are buoyant to output expansion and together account for two thirds of recurrent revenues. A continuous inflation in the 20 per cent range is presupposed in this package, which is aimed at keeping overall demand within but not far below feasible bounds.

In actual practice, policies along these lines are being pursued. No maxi has occurred although there was a rapid crawl in 1986 coupled with a midi-devaluation from 30 to 40 shillings to the dollar in June. Rough calculations suggest that real overvaluation relative to 1979 has been cut below 10 per cent. Promised net resource transfers are up to 150 per cent of visible exports of $350–400 million, so the external situation may work out. Tanzania's approach to donors stresses that foreign exchange is needed to cover operating costs and the rehabilitation of capital stock. It appears to be having a degree of success.

Ghana is going through a somewhat similar stabilization exercise, after almost two decades of economic and political dissolution. According to Reginald Green (1987) the economy was limited by shortages of both food and foreign exchange through this long period. The usual symptoms of parallel markets and corruption (or

---

[3] The additional policies are to avoid the worst stagflationary effects of devaluation. In Tanzania as in other countries that rely heavily on indirect taxes, the fiscal position should improve because taxes cascade on imports which enter at the 'bottom' of the production ladder. Reginald Green (in correspondence) estimates a 4.25 revenue multiplier on extra imports. Their local currency base automatically expands with depreciation (and growth).

'chopping off the backside') coupled with bribery (or 'dash') became endemic. Key prices, like the 1000 per cent overvalued exchange rate, were not so much wrong as irrelevant to economic calculation. Economic transactions passed beyond the ambit of official markets and the state.

A do-it-yourself attempt at stabilization under a reformist political regime failed in 1982, to be succeeded by a programme supported by the Bank and Fund in 1983–85. The results are illustrated in Table 5. The policies applied were off the shelf, except that enough foreign assistance was provided to permit imports to expand by 40 per cent over the three-year period.[4] Fiscal stringency was overdone, cutting into social services which were already at precarious levels. Officially recorded purchases and exports of cocoa recovered about 50 per cent over three years, although the relative contributions from re-routed smuggling and better weather are not clear.

Tight monetary policy embodied high interest rates, so high that enterprises did not wish to borrow and commercial banks (as in Tanzania) ended up excessively liquid. Bankers' doubts as to potential borrower solvency, their reluctance to accept high interest rate term deposits, and the breakdown of the system for payments by cheque exacerbated problems of savings mobilization and credit availability. Inflation dropped from 122 per cent in 1983 to 12 per cent in 1985, and rose again to about 25 per cent the following year. Part of this success was due to the inflow of imports and reorientation of foreign transactions from the parallel exchange rate to the newly realistic official one. However, the strongest single cause was the fall in food prices in 1984–85 resulting from a swing from severe drought to highly favourable weather. Flex-price responses applied at all levels of trade as wholesale and retail margins appear to have been squeezed along with grower prices. Indeed, generalized flex-price rules strongly assisted the monetarist anti-inflation cause.

The import surge involved an excess of non-essential (including consumer) goods. 'Somewhat ironically, the World Bank emerged as the temporary champion of a tough, prioritized centrally

---

[4] Gross resource transfers rose from $237 million in 1982 to an average of $588 million in 1983–85, with an upward trend.

Table. 5 Ghana: main economic indicators and sources and uses of foreign exchange

A: Main economic indicators (average annual change: %)

	Consumer price index	Real GDP Total	Per capita	Exports	Imports	Maize output
1980	50.1	1.2	−1.4	3.6	12.5	
1981	116.5	−3.8	−6.3	−35.6	5.1	−1
1982	22.3	−6.1	−8.5	−9.8	−38.2	−8
1983	121.9	−2.9	−5.4	−31.5	−1.8	−50
1984	40.2	7.6	5.0	28.9	23.2	233
1985 (est)[a]	20.0	5.3	2.6	7.8	18.0	−5

[a] CPI actual 12. GDP actual probably underestimated because 1.5 per cent food output growth estimate appears incompatible with 11 per cent food price decline and food exports.

B: Sources and uses of foreign exchange, 1983–85 (million $)

	Sources 1983	1984	1985		Uses 1983	1984	1985
Own sources							
Exports (fob)	439	566	610	Imports (fob)	500	616	727
Service (receipts)	39	49	38	Service payments	255	278	319
Total	478	615	648				
External sources				*Amortization*	124	115	236
Grants	61	125	88				
Long-term loans	84	133	200	Long-term loans	(69)	(50)	(33)
Medium-term loans	68	55	198	Medium-term loans	(55)	(65)	(203)
Private capital and transfers (net)	103	−17	88				

Table 5—*continued*

				Reduction in payments arrears	34	60	60
IMF disbursements	259	218	120	Others[a] (net)	170	60	0
Total	575	514	694				
Total resources	1053	1129	1342	*Total uses*	1053	1129	1342
Memo items: per cent increase in total resources	—	7	19				
Own sources as per cent of total resources	45	54	57				

[a] Includes movements in short-term monetary and non-monetary capital, change in official reserves, and errors and omissions.

operated forex/import licence allocation system . . .', according to Green. Later, the donor agencies swung behind a foreign exchange auction system installed in 1986 which seemed likely to direct imports further away from intermediates and capital goods. The bias will be especially strong if present limitations on the auction to intermediate and investment goods are phased out around 1988. The proposed changes would return Ghana to an open general licence for visible imports and allow free remittance of factor as well as service import payments.[5] The recent dominance of non-essential imports shows up in investment—despite a 10 per cent real

[5] A word is perhaps in order about foreign exchange auctions in general, since they figure in a number of recent stabilizations outside the WIDER sample. Green's view on Ghana and elsewhere is that auctions may depoliticize the exchange rate, but would be unlikely to do so if the auctioned and parallel rates took off together in a speculative bubble. Also, a thin, erratic market with a bias in favour of consumer imports is involved. 'Why frequent, small, technically determined [exchange rate] changes would not be superior in most contexts and a panacea in none is not at all self-evident.' We are back to the crawling peg.

GDP increase from 1982 to 1985, capital formation maintained at 8.5 per cent demand share.

In 1986 both domestic savings and investment rose as proportions of GDP while import volume grew less than expected, retail margins narrowed, and despite the introduction of the auction system the cost of living went up only about 25 per cent. The reason behind these favourable developments appears to have been overkill of personal income. Constant price personal consumption was virtually static, and may have fallen as much as 2.5 per cent in real per capita terms. This sluggishness of demand depressed margins, imports, and in some cases profits and production at significant social and political cost for no very evident economic gain. In 1984 and 1985 3 per cent or better per capita consumption increases had not led to overheating, and in 1986 GDP growth (despite the drag from consumer demand) was more than 5 per cent.

Green views the stabilization as a qualified success, with some difficulty in assigning the results among having a coherent policy, the specific programme adopted, better weather, and the capital inflows. Outstanding problems include cocoa (with several countries trying to expand production in the face of stable, price-inelastic world demand), promotion of other exports, and provision of inputs to agriculture and social services. 'Ghana suffers from adjustment fatigue . . . but will require capital inflows, avoidance of gimmickry, and sensible medium-term planning for the foreseeable future . . . A particular problem is the near total absence of the budgetary process as a resource-allocation and use-monitoring tool. It now serves only as a cash-flow control mechanism and prevents rather than facilitates achieving allocative efficiency at any level of recurrent budget spending.' As in Tanzania, local initiative and emphasis on non-price policies such as extension, research, and public investment to promote agriculture will be essential in the long haul. In the short run, the country's recent experience underlines the fact that orthodox stabilization-cum-liberalization packages can succeed when accompanied by substantial infusions of foreign exchange. But so can other sorts of programmes as well.

Sudan's economy combines the worst aspects of export dependence on a primary product—in this case labour—with what amounts to institutionalized capital flight. Conventional policy measures as applied in a series of Fund/Bank packages have effectively been beside the point. Indeed, by aborting local investment activity they may have exacerbated the difficulties of bringing foreign assets home for productive use.

John Harris (1986) sees domestic problems as beginning with the cessation of an investment boom around 1978. The idea propelling the boom was that Sudan would be transformed into the bread basket of the Middle East—most of the associated capital inflows came from oil-rich states in the region. The transformation failed, for reasons involving both technical difficulties and bad economic management of existing agricultural products. Traditional exports of cotton and other crops declined while cereals never made it into the picture. When capital inflows fell off along with the real price of oil after 1973, external strangulation of a fairly conventional sort apparently took over: inflationary, forced saving adjustment fattened traders' margins and measured GDP growth went flat.

Hidden behind domestic stagflation, however, is another story involving the national economy which in principle includes the income streams of Sudanese living abroad. According to field studies conducted by Nazli Choucri (1985) and Harris, about 310,000 emigrant workers in the Persian Gulf remit more than $9,000 each towards Sudan. Their supply-based estimate of the 1984 flow is $2.86 billion. This number dwarfs reported remittance inflows of $346 million in the balance of payments statistics, and in a couple of years could wipe out the official debt of $5.7 billion. What is the role of these payments in the domestic Sudanese economy?

Here the money trail becomes difficult to trace. Asset accumulation within Sudan apparently is substantial, involving real estate and the holdings of Levantine traders who may be opting out of Khartoum in the absence of local investment opportunities in the stagnant domestic system. The traders' presumably high saving flows (enhanced by inflationary income redistribution in their favour) are being channelled abroad and act as an exit vehicle for at least part of the remittances entering the country. Another parcel may leave in the form of asset accumulation outside Sudan by the military. Meanwhile both the 'official' and productive sectors of the economy are starved of foreign exchange, provoking austere IMF policies which among other politically visible effects led to food riots in 1985 when consumer subsidies were cut. The implication is that a large proportion of the hard currency flows pass through

Sudan like the physicists' neutrinos, perhaps leaving a shell of 'informal' Sudanese pound-denominated liabilities (the domestic assets of the remittors) which is not visible in the official financial statistics. Most of the dollars ultimately end up as assets of someone (not necessarily their original senders) in North Atlantic money markets or elsewhere in the Middle East in forms like Egyptian real estate.

The domestic policy issue resembles one in countries subject to large capital flights such as Argentina and Mexico (see below). Extensive private sector external assets coexist with public liabilities, in Sudan's case left over from the investment boom and ex-President Nimeiri's manipulations thereafter. How public and enterprise penury can be remedied by private wealth transfers is the problem. By themselves, purely market-oriented incentives such as a weak exchange rate and high deposit interest rates in Khartoum are not likely to resolve it. Renewed domestic growth which would open up productive investment opportunities within the country might be a partial solution, but it cannot be tried if conventional austerity policies continue to be applied.

4.2 Foreign Bonanzas, Short and Long Run

The economies analyzed in this section share external dependence with those just discussed, but have been luckier in foreign commodity and capital markets, at least at times. They are also larger, richer, and have taken industrialization further. We begin with Colombia and Mexico, where fluctuations in foreign receipts over periods of a few years have been important, and go on to Egypt and the Philippines which in some ways have suffered from a surfeit of dollars of geopolitical origin for too long.

Colombia has long been a major coffee exporter. Its regulatory agency, the National Coffee Fund, is operated by the private Federation of coffee-growers. In the past, the Fund has not completely buffered coffee revenue fluctuations—they have had significant macro and distributional effects. Other important sectors include flex-price food agriculture and fix-price urban activities. Distribution and demand patterns are such that a drop in food production leads to overall contraction. The economy is also stagnationist in that reductions in mark-up rates (which occurred during recession in the mid-1980s) stimulate demand. Intersectoral income linkages are quite complex. Table 6 provides an illustration, along with data on recent stabilization experiences.

Non-coffee exports have traditionally been supported by a variety of policies, including the invention in the late 1960s of the crawling peg. Nonetheless, their share in GDP has declined slowly over time. Imports are mostly complementary to domestic activity, and regulated by tariffs and quotas. There are reasonably effective exchange controls. Fiscal policy has been prudent, with no big deficits appearing. To an extent, the traditional agro-exporter model applies in that coffee price fluctuations are partly offset by changes in public investment and National Coffee Fund financial adjustment.

Recent stabilizations originated from a coffee price bonanza in the mid-1970s. The demand surge from incomplete buffering of the revenues was partly offset by tight monetary regulation. High reserve requirements and similar policies led to a proliferation of non-bank financial intermediaries. As restrictions relaxed when the boom ended, these new entities were left unregulated and fragile.

In 1980–82 recession set in. Coffee revenues were off, while real appreciation and liberalization aimed at controlling inflation cut back on other exports and let in a flood of imports. The current account gap rose by more than the consolidated fiscal deficit, including output contraction. The weak financial intermediaries began to fail. The first step of a new government in late 1982 was to bail out the financial system by nationalizing some intermediaries and cleaning up the balance sheets of others with rediscount operations. The presence of exchange controls helped prevent these local financial jitters from spilling over into capital flight.

The next step was to institute a rather heterodox policy line based on tight import controls, tax increases to balance the fiscal budget, and a faster crawl. The controls were the active element. The improvement in external balance they induced was matched internally by the other policies in a generally successful programme.

This package was overlaid in 1984–86 by more orthodox policies at the urging of the Bank (with which Colombia has had a long-term 'special relationship') and Fund. Liberalization, faster depreciation, and austerity did not turn out to be as stagflationary as expected, largely because there were favourable agricultural conditions and mark-ups declined. Whether or not the pro-cyclical

Table 6 Colombia: social income matrix, major macroeconomic indicators, and balance of payments

A: Social income matrix, 1980

	Coffee	Raw materials	Food stuffs	Minerals	Urban goods	Govern-ment	Total GDP	Direct tax payments (−) receipts (+)	Total GDP after direct tax payments
Distribution of gross production value [a]									
Rural workers	21.5	12.0	11.3	0.1	0.6	0.0	5.2		4.9
Urban workers	8.6	9.3	5.4	18.7	35.9	0.0	26.4	−0.6	25.8
Bureaucrats	0.0	0.0	0.0	0.0	0.0	99.2	7.9	−0.2	7.7
Peasants	8.0	4.5	8.4	0.0	0.2	0.0	3.0		2.9
Rural rentiers	5.3	30.2	47.7	0.2	1.6	0.0	14.8	−0.1	14.7
Capitalists	9.3	34.1	21.2	54.8	41.2	0.0	33.8 [b]	−2.5	31.3
Indirect taxes	44.0	2.3	1.3	14.4	8.0	0.8	8.9 [c]	3.3	12.2
Intermediate imports	3.3	8.2	4.0	11.8	12.6	0.0			
Total	100.0	100.0	100.0	100.0	100.0	100.0	100.0		100.0
Share in									
Final demand	6.4	2.1	23.4	2.0	59.0	7.1			
Total demand	4.7	3.9	14.6	5.0	66.6	5.2			
Value added at factor cost	4.5	5.4	24.4	4.2	52.9	8.6			

[a] All shares include direct and indirect participation of each cost or income in the total value of gross production by sector.

[b] Includes importers' trading margins on imports of final goods.

[c] Includes duties on imports of final goods.

Table 6—*continued*

B: Major macroeconomic indicators, 1980–85

	1980	1981	1982	1983	1984	1985	1980–85
Production growth (%)							
Total GDP	4.1	2.3	0.9	1.0	3.2	2.0	1.9
Manufacturing	1.2	−2.6	−1.4	0.5	8.0	3.0	1.4
Agriculture	2.2	3.2	−1.9	1.8	1.1	1.8	1.2
Other	6.1	3.9	3.0	1.2	2.2	1.8	2.3
Fiscal deficit (% of GDP)							
National government	2.8	3.7	4.5	4.1	4.0	1.4	
National government, excluding interest payments	2.3	3.0					
Consolidated public sector, except coffee fund	4.6	5.4	7.5	7.6	7.5	5.7	
Coffee fund	−1.3	0.9	0.6	0.8			
Total consolidated	3.3	6.3	8.1	8.0			
Employment (1980=100)							
Secondary sector	100.0	98.9	99.4	102.6	106.9	109.5	
Tertiary sector	100.0	105.2	109.9	115.0	119.3	124.2	
Wage labourers	100.0	105.5	107.4	108.4	109.6	112.9	
Self-employed	100.0	103.8	109.9	119.0	125.9	131.2	
Rate of unemployment (%)	9.7	8.3	9.1	11.8	13.1	14.0	
Average real earnings (1980=100)							
Private employees	100.0	103.9	106.1	109.6	111.6	112.7	
Public employees	100.0	103.8	107.9	115.1	119.8	121.7	
Self-employed	100.0	113.7	114.5	110.4	100.4	103.2	
Inflation (end of year, %)	26.0	26.3	24.0	16.6	18.3	22.5	

Table 6—*continued*

C: Balance of payments, 1980–85 (million dollars, net balances)

	1980	1981	1982	1983	1984	1985
Current account	104	−1722	−2885	−2826	−2050	−1220
Trade balance[a]	13	−1333	−2076	−1317	−404	149
Non-financial services and transfers	302	38	−22	−591	−406	−15
Financial services	−211	−427	−787	−918	−1240	−1354
Capital account[b]	985	2009	2235	1436	944	1850
Direct investment	48	226	330	512	558	728
Long-term financing	807	1384	1290	1016	1264	1330
Short-term capital	130	399	615	−92	878	−208
Other[c]	−16	55	−4	−67	20	−39
Errors and omissions	162	−100	−47	−266	−175	−307
Global balance	1235	242	−701	−1723	−1261	284

[a] Includes non-monetary gold.
[b] Excluding contributions to international organizations.
[c] Contributions to international organizations and counterpart items.

mark-up squeeze will reverse in the future remains an open question.

Eduardo Lora and Jose Antonio Ocampo (1986), the authors of the Colombia paper, feel that the 1980–82 policy did not go far enough. Imports should have been controlled more effectively and public investment redirected to the domestic market when coffee prices began to go down. Other resource balance problems will arise in the near future. Returns from coffee and the expansion of oil and coal exports (production capacity courtesy of public investment programmes throughout the 1980s), magnified by real devaluation, will generate domestic surpluses. What should be the policy response? One issue is new investment in coffee. The authors feel that capacity expansion is likely to be counter-productive.

Second, how much of the proceeds from real devaluation should be transmitted to the growers and how much sterilized by the state? An excessive pass-through will stimulate inflation based in the first instance on food flex-prices. An offsetting contractionary policy would be required. Sterilization can help the wealth position of growers (they would be given interest-bearing foreign deposits at the central bank), and would not require contractionary policy. Well-directed public investment would 'socialize' some of the proceeds of coffee and coal. How feasible such a policy will be is unclear—the coffee Federation has a short time horizon and a great deal of political clout.

Mexico's economy resembles Colombia's in that there is a large fix-price, demand-adjusting component. Internal food prices, however, are linked to the international market (though the state has traditionally intervened to keep them stable). Urban wage formation is heavily influenced by the government, which after 50 years of domination by one political party—the PRI—impinges upon all spheres of the economy. Rural wages are closer to being market-clearing, but are affected by possibilities for migration to the US. The financial system is heavily 'dollarized'. Because of a fairly open capital market on the one hand, and large state interest-bearing debt obligations on the other, the interest rate can only be pegged within a narrow band. Credit (and money) supply becomes correspondingly endogenous.

According to Nora Lustig and Jaime Ros (1987), Mexico went through a boom period in 1978–81 after the massive oil discoveries a couple of years before. An EFF stabilization agreed to with the IMF in 1976 was quietly dropped. However, rapid growth, real exchange appreciation under inflation, and (especially) the massive debt built up in the late 1970s set the stage for an extremely orthodox stabilization attempt after the financial crisis in August 1982. Contributing to the collapse was capital flight (more than $20 billion), fed by state borrowing to support the exchange rate and the accumulation of dollar liabilities by firms. Comparative data on the stabilizations in the mid-1970s and early 1980s appear in Table 7.

The second episode went through three phases: a shock treatment in 1983, gradualism in 1984 to mid-1985, and then a shock again. The initial package involved reducing the fiscal deficit by half,[6] splitting the exchange rate (with the more depreciated one for capital movements and tourism) and devaluing both rates, and cutting back 100 per cent wage indexation to past inflation by the same 50 per cent. Business balance sheets were cleaned up with rediscount operations through which the government assumed most of the foreign debt. Credit ceilings turned out to be inoperative, since firms did not borrow and the banking system ended up with excess reserves.

The outcomes in 1983 included a 5 per cent decline in real GDP, as opposed to a projected output loss of zero. The trade surplus went to $14 billion, more than twice as much as required for debt service. The target for the fiscal deficit was satisfied, but inflation was 80 per cent instead of the projected 55 per cent. What went wrong? Lustig and Ross point to three main factors.

First, the IMF/government team used the wrong inflation model, counting on significantly slower price increases to be induced by trade liberalization and austerity. Inflation did not decelerate, leading to 20–30 per cent real wage losses and a reduced real demand injection from the fiscal deficit.

Second, the designers of the package underestimated the short-run contractionary (and inflationary) effects of devaluation.

Third, they did not take into account the dependence of private capital formation on public investment and overall output in an accelerator response. Mexico has not pursued import substitution of capital goods, so much of the trade improvement came from

[6] In line with the sharecropper's traditional fraction of the harvest, the Fund often tries to extract 'excess' from deficits in portions of 50 per cent.

Table 7 Mexico: the economy in two stabilization periods

	1976	1977	1978	1981	1982	1983	1984	1985
Gross domestic product (growth %)	4.2	3.4	8.1	7.9	−0.5	−5.3	3.7	2.7
Total consumption	4.7	1.7	7.2	7.7	1.2	−6.8	3.0	2.0
Private consumption	4.5	2.0	6.9	7.3	1.1	−7.5	2.5	2.1
Public consumption	6.4	−1.1	9.7	10.1	2.3	−1.3	6.8	1.3
Total investment	0.4	−6.7	15.4	14.7	−15.9	−27.9	5.1	6.7
Private investment	6.1	−6.7	4.7	13.9	−17.3	−24.2	9.0	13.1
Public investment	−7.6	−6.7	33.0	15.8	−14.2	−32.5	0.6	−3.1
Exports	16.6	14.7	17.4	6.2	13.7	11.5	10.5	−3.0
Imports	1.0	−10.2	18.6	20.3	−37.1	−41.7	19.7	11.8
Inflation (%)	15.0	28.9	17.5	28.0	58.9	101.9	65.5	57.7
Nominal exchange rate (controlled) (pesos per dollar)	—	—	—	—	57.0	121.2	169.6	257.0
Nominal exchange rate (free) (pesos per dollar)	15.4	22.6	22.8	23.8	92.7	150.8	187.2	310.2
Nominal minimum wages (growth %)	29.2	27.9	6.6	31.3	40.7	66.3	39.7	37.05
Nominal average wages (growth %)	29.7	24.7	18.7	33.4	55.1	48.5	57.4	n.a.
Real exchange rate (controlled) 1978=100	—	—	—	—	128.4	130.1	112.2	116.2
Real exchange rate (free) 1978=100	96.8	106.4	100.0	79.8	208.8	161.8	123.7	140.03
Real minimum wages (growth %)	11.6	−8.1	−1.2	2.6	−11.5	−16.9	−6.7	−1.2
Real average wages (growth %)	12.0	−3.3	1.0	4.2	−2.4	−26.5	−4.9	n.a.
Trade balance (billion dollars)	−2.0	0.0	−0.5	−5.3	5.4	14.4	13.8	8.8
Current account balance (billion dollars)	−3.7	−1.6	−2.7	−12.5	−4.9	5.3	4.2	0.5

decreased imports for investment demand. The collapse would have been worse, had not consumption in a stagnationist economy been supported to an extent by a wealth effect. Devaluation increased the local currency value of flown capital, and probably stimulated some purchases within Mexico.

In the gradualist phase, increases in wages, the exchange rate, and public enterprise prices were geared to stabilize inflation. With some real appreciation, it seemed to settle at 50 plus per cent per year. Import liberalization (Mexico traditionally had a strong quota system and low tariffs), the initial devaluations, a fast depreciation write-off to stimulate investment, dropping export subsidies, and high interest rates were supposed to act together in creating conditions for higher saving and export increases to bring the economy back to positive growth.

To judge by official pronouncements, equalization of incentives to get 'little triangle' welfare gains and faith in a neoclassical savings-driven growth model were the intellectual foundations for these policy moves.[7] Unsurprisingly they had scant effect. The only apparently favourable change was some recovery in the car industry as businesses took advantage of the depreciation write-offs to renovate their fleets. For the rest, in 1984–85 there was an increasing gap between the projected and actual inflation rates. Trade targets were not met, as the 1983 external improvement proved to be evanescent.

Appreciation in 1984 was apparently undertaken for fear of excess demand inflation. Capacity utilization was low but the money supply had risen as reserves built up from the trade surplus. The stronger peso led to expansion and the favourable trade position melted. Renewed doubts about being able to meet debt payments and the worldwide oil price decreases in 1985–86 set off another austerity/devaluation shock that extended into 1987. Over all this time, non-oil exports never did respond much to the 33 per cent real depreciation (compared to 1981) that stayed in force. Complementary industrial policy and public investment to push

[7] Welfare gains in the standard neoclassical approach are illustrated in diagrams by areas between supply and demand curves on one side of the point where they cross. The regions are triangular; hence the reference in the text. As usually computed, benefits from removing distortions amount to small fractions of GDP. One is entitled to doubts as to their practical relevance.

exports were conspicuously lacking. The only sub-sectors that grew (by a billion dollars or so) were the *maquiladora* assembly operations along the US border.

Looking back, Lustig and Ros observe that much of the overkill might have been avoided by less draconian wage and fiscal spending cuts. The GDP losses Mexico endured were far greater than the amounts required to service debt, while cancelled investment programmes do not bode well for long-term recovery. In the future, debt relief (or veiled repudiation) and a more egalitarian distributional policy supported by state initiative to rebuild industry and exports will be essential. One relatively bright spot is agriculture, which benefited from good weather and high internal food prices tied to devaluation. Continued success in the sector could support modest expansion in the rest of the economy.

The Philippines effectively had a foreign bonanza between 1970 and 1983, under a seemingly endless sequence of IMF stand-by agreements. Capital inflows were large enough to permit 18 per cent real appreciation over the period, with modest diversification from primary exports into low value-added assembly of garments and semi-conductor products. Green Revolution technology offset by adverse agricultural terms-of-trade movements left the nation marginally self-sufficient in rice (an improvement over the rice trade deficit prior to 1970). Import substitution created an oligopolistic industrial sector dependent on intermediate imports.

The stage was set for crisis when the Marcos regime engaged in massive borrowing to finance investment projects in the late 1970s. They largely failed, leaving foreign obligations which were assumed by the state. The interest payments were increasingly covered by high-cost, short-term commercial bank loans from abroad in classic Ponzi fashion. The game broke down in mid-1983 when banks refused to roll over their credits. Several maxi-devaluations followed, increasing the local currency value of the interest obligations the state had taken over. (The central bank outlay became the biggest deficit item in the consolidated government accounts.) Protracted negotiations with the Fund finally led to the eighteenth Philippino stand-by at the end of 1984.[8] During that

[8] The delay in signing a stand-by came from several causes, notably press leaks in December 1983, of the fact that the central bank had been overstating its reserves since 1981, and the government's preoccupation with election campaigning until June 1984.

year, however, steps towards stabilization were taken, apparently with tacit support and approval from the IMF.

As interpreted by Manual Montes (1987), government concerns centred on short-term finance and politics. With regard to the former, negotiations in wake of the Fund agreement produced credit lines worth about $3 billion in 1985. To assure the outcomes of 'election exercises' carried out to please the Americans, the government undertook major spending programmes in late 1983/ early 1984, and again a year later. How these activities were to fit into an IMF-type austerity programme makes an interesting tale.

The manoeuvre Marcos and his advisors adopted was to have the central bank borrow from the rest of the financial system to pay for the campaigns under a high interest-rate regime. Through 'Jobo bills', 'reverse repurchase agreements', and other devices, several per cent of GDP were transferred from the private sector bank credit to the state.[9] As depositors pulled their money from bank accounts to buy the central bank paper, there was substantial disintermediation. The ratio of banking system liquidity to the money base dropped by 30 per cent between mid-1983 and mid-1984. The credit squeeze made interest rates shoot up from 15 per cent at the end of 1983 to 45 per cent a year later. Figures 2A and 2B illustrate the close links between the liquidity crunch and real output, while Table 8 provides additional data on the stabilization period.

Cost-push from these high rates plus nominal devaluation drove inflation to 63 per cent per year during the third quarter of 1984, and induced GDP decreases of 6.8 and 3.8 per cent in 1984 and 1985 respectively. Nonetheless, austerity forced inflation down to single digit rates by late 1985 and made the trade balance slightly positive. What were the reasons for the 'success'?

Montes notes several factors. First, wage-setting and other price adjustments in the Philippines are not indexed, so that monetarist inflation theory applies in that aggregate demand reduction does slow price increases. However, cost pressures caused the 1983 inflation spike and could underlie longer duration propagation mechanisms in the future. As in Mexico, the trade balance

[9] The bills were popularly christened in honour of the central bank governor's nickname. The bank was obliged by custom to buy back its maturing obligations. Reversing such a repurchase amounted to rolling over its debt to the private sector.

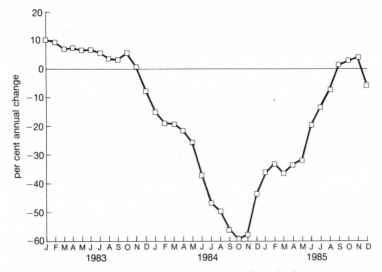

Fig. 2A. The Philippines: real liquidity of the banking system

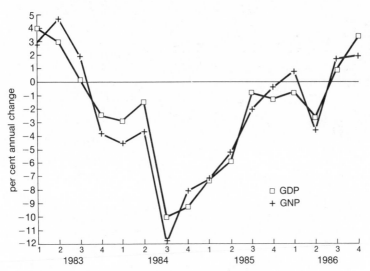

Fig. 2B. The Philippines: GNP and GNP growth rates

Table 8 The Philippines: real macroeconomic variables

Quarter	Personal consumption	Government consumption	Gross dom. capital formation	Fixed capital formation	Total construction	Government construction	Private construction	Exports	Imports	GDP	GNP
1982/1	14265	2199	7237	5751	2956	1274	1682	4352	4815	24285	24157
1982/2	15519	2262	6415	5875	3326	1488	1838	4585	4800	24967	24616
1982/3	15741	2290	6852	6213	2980	1252	1728	4336	4980	22927	22468
1982/4	18010	2394	5763	5848	3259	1345	1914	4477	4872	26820	26290
1983/1	14837	2276	6981	5873	3148	1234	1914	4459	4344	25251	24838
1983/2	15898	2311	7098	6426	3832	1708	2124	5090	4968	25706	25763
1983/3	16087	2197	5378	5578	2423	533	1890	4819	4913	22960	22878
1983/4	18256	2004	5572	5135	2545	900	1645	4317	4966	26151	25288
1984/1	15021	2242	4653	4732	2968	990	1978	4621	3940	24519	23707
1984/2	16073	2117	4563	4477	2817	924	1893	5048	4323	25314	24822
1984/3	16241	2003	3286	3767	1929	482	1447	5482	4821	20655	20165
1984/4	18698	1893	3349	3565	1732	589	1143	5695	5091	23728	23239
1985/1	15144	2055	3446	3400	1986	678	1308	5088	3224	22725	21994
1985/2	16088	2027	3502	3793	2432	837	1595	4880	3678	23818	23520
1985/3	16240	2052	2719	3280	1842	617	1225	4823	3791	20479	19750
1985/4	18690	2071	2898	2241	648	210	438	4560	3302	23422	23143
1986/1	15343	2131	3261	3192	1794	879	915	5114	3634	22549	22164
1986/2	16174	1976	2177	2362	948	415	533	6516	4432	23196	22679
1986/3	16248	2103	2741	2861	1407	767	640	6127	4220	20660	20089
1986/4	18913	2170	2507	2284	834	283	551	5846	4193	24200	23593

improved mostly from reductions in demand for imported interme-diates and (especially) capital goods. Exports did not rise, nor do they seem likely to in the wake of renewed real appreciation as the maxi-devaluations erode.

Even within Marcos's political context, Montes argues that the stabilization could have been done in more gradualistic fashion: in particular, targets in 1985 were far too tough after 1984. Trade improvement could have been achieved more effectively with directed incentives to exports and small-scale import substitution as opposed to maxi-devaluations. According to simulations based on a rather monetarist econometric model, gradualism could have offset the major GDP losses which occurred with $1 billion or so of higher payments deficits. Such manoeuvres would have been possible since only $1.25 billion of the $3 billion credit line negotiated after the 1984 IMF stand-by was actually spent. Towards the future, steps will have to be taken to stimulate exports, foment capital formation, and generally restore the private sector ravaged by Marcos's manipulations and the subsequent stabiliza-tion package.

Egypt's external account history in some ways parallels that of the Philippines. A stabilization effort was underway in 1977, but was soon forgotten after oil price increases, emigrant remittances, Suez canal revenues, tourism, and (above all) the Camp David accords opened the gates to enough foreign exchange to permit domestic absorption to exceed GDP by upwards of 15 per cent. Table 9 illustrates the magnitude of the resource transfers involved.

The absence of exchange pressures for a decade permitted the Egyptian economy to retain the structure it built up in the 1950s—price and quantity regulation of the industrial sector by the state, ample public employment, widespread food subsidies, and a relatively egalitarian income distribution. Exchange management has traditionally taken the form of a multiple rate structure, and the financial system is highly dollarized. Because of limitations on arable land (six million Nile Valley acres for 50 million people), the country is a net food importer. However, agricultural productivity is high, and the diverse crop mix responds to price signals (though of course overall agricultural output in the short run cannot). Regulated prices for production inputs and consumer food purchases have long been a sore point between Egypt and its aid

Table 9 Egypt: balance of payments on capital account, 1974–1983/84 (million $US)

	1974	1975	1976	1977	1978	1979	1980/81	1981/82	1982/83	1983/84*
I. Current account balance	−1596	−2426	−1363	−1456	−1361	−1915	−2348	−3501	−2715	−3299
II. Autonomous capital flows	156	495	1091	1207	1528	2527	2280	2315	2512	2928
direct investment	87	225	444	477	387	1375	836	885	966	897
official loans (net)	−21	210	490	803	1028	890	1220	1385	1257	1762
private loans (net)	90	59	157	−73	113	262	224	45	289	269
III. Balance on autonomous transactions	−1440	−1931	−272	−249	167	612	−68	−1186	−203	−371
IV. Medium-term BOP financing	1261	1506	780	1601	809	72	—	—	—	—
grants	1261	986	705	382	291	72	—	—	—	—
loans	—	520	75	1219	518	—	—	—	—	—
V. Balance on non-monetary transactions	−179	−425	508	1352	976	684	−68	−1186	−203	371

* Estimated.

donors. The riots of January 1977 in response to Bretton Woods pressures to remove food subsidies remain vivid in the national political memory.

The external situation worsened markedly in 1985–86 as oil and remittance inflows fell and debt obligations for defence purchases came due. A mini financial crisis may be in the making because the authorities tapped reserves for foreign currency deposits in the banking system to pay for imports during 1986. An agreement was signed with the IMF in mid-1987, featuring unification and devaluation of the multiple rate system (with a crawling dual rate at the top), austerity, and pressures from liberalization and getting prices right. As a consequence, Gouda Abdel-Khalek (1987) fears overkill, for example from the contractionary forces implicit in raising internal energy prices, reducing food subsidies, and devaluation. Interest rate increases are also likely to feed through into cost-push. Gradualism and utilizing directed policies to avoid major recession are his preferred policy recommendations. In the long run, planned rationalization of the mode of production in both agriculture and industry will be required.

4.3 Redistribution and Liberalization Experiments

Stabilizations involving liberalization coupled with apparently planned, regressive changes in income distribution have played out in Turkey, Sri Lanka, and Chile (from the most to least successful cases) over the past decade. These programmes, all undertaken with Fund or Bank collaboration, are discussed in this section.

Turkey, around 1960, entered into a period of import substitution based on public sector investment which by 1980 had resulted in a diversified industrial base. There was steady growth in real wages and peasant remunerations, supporting demand in a stagnationist economy. But by the late 1970s, an increasing profit squeeze and external shocks forced the economic model to break down. Political leaders in fear of losing their grip pushed expansionary policies when a degree of austerity would have been appropriate, leading to an inflation rate exceeding 100 per cent in 1980. In September of that year, a military coup transformed an on-going dialogue with the IMF into a stabilization programme of far-reaching scope. Its outcomes are illustrated in Table 10.

According to Korkut Boratav (1986), the programme was not

Table 10 Turkey: macroeconomic indicators and balance of payments

A: Some macro-economic indicators, 1977–1984

	1977	1978	1979	1980	1981	1982	1983	1984
I. Growth rates[a] (%)								
a. GDP[b]	4.9	4.4	−0.4	−1.0	4.7	4.3	4.1	5.8
b. Agricul.	0.4	2.7	2.8	1.7	0.0	6.3	0.0	3.8
c. Industry	13.8	6.6	−5.4	−5.6	7.4	4.5	8.0	9.1
d. Services	3.3	4.0	0.2	−0.2	5.7	3.3	4.3	5.2
II. GDP per capita (index)[c]	100.0	102.2	100.0	96.7	98.9	100.6	102.2	106.1
III. Relative sectoral price indices								
a. Industry/services	100.0	104.9	111.2	126.4	129.3	131.7	134.9	136.4
b. Agricul./services	100.0	87.0	75.1	73.6	75.3	69.0	68.2	70.1
IV. Shares in GNP (%)								
a. Savings[d]	18.0	15.9	16.2	15.9	18.0	18.2	16.5	16.6
i. public	6.3	5.3	2.7	5.3	8.6	9.0	7.3	5.3
ii. private	11.7	10.6	13.5	10.6	9.4	9.2	9.2	11.3
b. Investment[e]	25.6	22.4	21.7	19.7	19.3	19.0	19.0	16.7
V. Rate of inflation[f]	24.0	52.7	63.9	107.3	36.8	25.2	30.6	52.0

Notes:
[a] In constant 1968 prices.
[b] At factor cost.
[c] The service sector is defined as GDP—agriculture—industry.
[d] In current prices.
[e] Fixed capital formation in constant 1983 prices.
[f] Wholesale prices of Ministry of Commerce.

Relative sectoral prices are calculated from GDP implicit price deflators.

Table 10—*continued*

B: Main components of balance of payments, 1973–84 (millions of dollars)

	1973	1977	1978	1979	1980	1981	1982	1983	1984
Exports	1317	1753	2288	2261	2910	4703	5746	5728	7134
Imports	-2086	-5796	-4599	-5069	-7909	-8933	-8843	-9235	-10757
Trade balance	*-769*	*-4043*	*-2311*	*-2808*	*-4999*	*-4230*	*-3097*	*-3507*	*-3623*
Interest on debt	-59	-320	-389	-546	-668	-1193	-1465	-1442	-1607
Workers' remittances	1183	982	983	1694	2071	2490	2187	1554	1881
Other invisibles (net)	129	-4	299	552	501	965	1223	1272	1409
Current acc. balance	*484*	*-3385*	*-1418*	*-1108*	*-3095*	*-1968*	*-1152*	*-2123*	*-1940*
Capital movements	*433*	*1517*	*1202*	*434*	*2672*	*1136*	*1428*	*1562*	*1827*
debt repayment	-72	-214	-256	-544	-575	-551	-852	-1093	-1278
direct investment	79	67	47	85	33	44	41	72	207
proj. and prog. credits	376	502	560	1068	2391	1482	1761	1117	1498
IMF	—	—	170	30	488	359	205	193	-68
others (net)	50	1162	681	-205	335	-198	273	1273	1467
Reserves	-728	-565	-158	-111	-607	-184	-482	-52	-1457
Errors and omissions	-189	2433	374	785	1030	1016	206	613	1570

monetarist in the usual sense—money supply accommodated to nominal GDP growth over the 1980–83 period. Subsidies for exports through tax rebates and favourable interest rates were another unorthodox feature. However, the package did incorporate positive real interest rates, a maxi-devaluation followed by a crawling peg, import liberalization, and substantial balance of payments support.[10] It was distributionally regressive, embodying real wage cuts of 20–30 per cent in comparison to 1979. The terms of trade shifted against peasants, due to the removal of support prices and declining demand. The outcome was a sizeable drop in domestic consumer purchases.

Other aspects of the exercise included a national financial crisis in 1981 which did not, however, spill over into capital flight on a grand scale. This risk was probably averted by high local interest rates and the crawling peg (though these policies, of course, tempted firms to borrow abroad). The crisis was suffocated with the usual bail outs of the balance sheets of the 'formal' affected banks; informal money merchants did not fare so well. Inflation settled back to an annual rate of 30–40 per cent (though it rose again in 1984 to 50 per cent), fed by cost push from the interest and exchange rates. Finally, capital formation, traditionally in the range of one-quarter of GDP, fell steadily to less than 17 per cent in 1984. The previous motors for private investment—planned public projects and accelerator linkages within the economy—vanished with the stabilization.

The major success of the programme was an explosion of exports, from 5.1 per cent of GDP in 1980 to 14.3 per cent in 1984, with a big manufactured component. The reasons for this development are diverse. The existing industrial base provided the foundation, while the distributional shifts cut back on domestic demand. Price incentives (devaluation and 25 to 30 per cent export subsidies) no doubt played a role. Finally, external demand conditions in Turkey's part of the world were favourable. Four neighbours (Iraq, Iran, Libya, and Saudi Arabia) had their share of exports rise from less than 10 per cent in 1979 to 34 per cent in 1983 and 31 per cent in 1984. This apparent demand stagnation, plus the low level of investment, suggests that the export boom may be nearing its limits

[10] The trade deficit went from $2.8 billion in 1979 to $5.0 and $4.2 billion in 1980 and 1981 respectively before dropping back to the $3.5 billion range. Similar movements also characterized the current account.

in terms of both markets to penetrate and local capacity to produce. Preliminary recent data are consistent with this view, showing that exports continued to increase through 1985 but declined by $500 million in 1986, while the trade deficit held stable and the current account deficit widened from $1.2 to $1.8 billion. In anticipation of elections in 1987 or 1988, public investment did increase in 1986, largely for municipal infrastructure projects sponsored by the ruling party. Their import content helped keep open the trade gap.

Looking at the past, one might ask whether the programme could have been done better, given the amounts of foreign resources provided. (Whether such a question makes political sense is another matter.) Boratav observes that better distribution and fewer consumer goods imports (which increased their share in the growing import total by 3 per cent) were feasible, in principle permitting more local production for consumption and capital stock growth. In the future he sees a need for reactivating productive investment by public policy, the strengthening of tentative recent steps towards moderating the incomes policy by going in the direction of collective bargaining and wage indexation, a reduction in interest rates, and a degree of exchange appreciation coupled with export subsidies (or perhaps dual rates). If there is no repudiation of payments on the country's $30 billion external debt, capital inflows will have to continue for a long time.

Sri Lanka's history of stabilization resembles Turkey's in its distributional aspects, although the island's economy is more like those of the small, externally strangled countries discussed in Section 4.1. The main exports are tea, rubber, and coconut products which have suffered the same unfavourable price trends as other primary commodities. The manufacturing sector is small (about 15 per cent of GDP) and agricultural processing is a major activity. Rice paddy farmers are a major component of the social matrix. The 'poor' are politically visible. Sri Lanka has social welfare indicators (literacy, life expectancy, etc.) far above those of other countries at its level of per capital income. This achievement was made possible in part by an extensive food subsidy programme, amounting to 21 per cent of current public expenditure and 5 per cent of GDP in 1978. In the same year, other social programmes accounted for 15 per cent of spending and 4 per cent of GDP.

As recounted by Lal Jayawardena, Anne Maasland, and P. N.

Radhakrishnan (1988), a stabilization programme was put in place late in 1977 when a new government took office in a political shift away from a populist regime which had expansionary dreams but great difficulties in obtaining foreign resources. The old government had undertaken a nominal 20 per cent currency appreciation as an anti-inflationary device in the face of monetary expansion in the order of 30 per cent from the fiscal deficit and an unsterilized reserve increase from a short-lived boom in tea prices. How the programme fared on the basis of these initial conditions is summarized in Table 11.

Devaluation, as usual, figured in the stabilization package. In the Sri Lankan case it had notable effects. At the time, the country was a net rice importer, and the new government felt that producer prices had to be increased to encourage supply. By keeping higher farmgate prices off the government's subsidy books, depreciation turned out to be central to the stabilization effort.[11] The package also included fiscal deficit reduction, import liberalization, unification of the dual exchange rate, and external support from the Bretton Woods agencies and other donors.

One part of the austerity—forced by the rice producer price increases together with a limitation on the fiscal deficit—was replacement of quantity distribution of subsidized rice by food stamps *not* indexed to inflation. There is substantial debate as to which price index 'correctly' measures inflation, but the food component of the Colombo consumer price index rose by 29 and 18 per cent in 1980 and 1981 respectively. These increases were enough to reduce food stamp transfers and subsidies to 8.7 per cent of current government spending by 1982. With such a cut, the nutritional status of poorer segments of the population appears to be deteriorating at a steady pace.

Overall inflation stabilized at 17 per cent by 1984 (18 per cent for food) 1.5 times the rate of the previous decade. Capital inflows which let imports in the early 1980s run about 30 per cent above their levels in 1978 helped in this accomplishment, as well as permitting officially reported GDP growth to rise from 3 to 5 per cent. The authors argue that this last figure may be overestimated

[11] Recall from Section 4.1 that a weak exchange rate plays a similar role with respect to the balance sheets of export marketing boards when they try to support high producer prices.

Table 11 Sri Lanka: GDP accounts and balance of payments

A: Growth rates of GDP and its components, 1978–84[a] (Rs million at constant 1970 factor prices)

	1978	1979	1980	1981	1982	1983[b]	1984[b]
Agriculture[c]	4,532	4,622	4,766	5,097	5,231	5,508	5,624
Mining	619	652	684	713	742	800	808
Manufacturing	2,541	2,659	2,681	2,820	2,955	2,979	3,319
Construction	794	960	1,066	1,034	1,013	1,023	1,023
Services	8,915	9,608	10,378	11,042	11,815	12,595	13,326
utilities	158	190	209	234	257	274	282
transport/communications	1,607	1,716	1,838	1,957	2,079	2,173	2,282
commercial services	3,267	3,551	3,849	4,034	4,275	4,502	4,835
financial services	318	350	402	462	517	628	697
housing services	499	518	549	579	611	623	635
public administration	854	905	959	997	1,102	1,439	1,583
other services	2,212	2,378	2,572	2,779	2,974	2,965	2,995
Gross domestic product	17,401	18,501	19,575	20,706	21,756	22,844	23,986
Annual growth rate (%)							
Agriculture[c]	5.4	2.0	3.1	6.9	2.6	5.3	2.1
Mining	20.2	5.3	4.9	4.2	4.1	7.8	1.0
Manufacturing	7.8	4.6	0.8	5.2	4.8	0.8	11.4
Construction	28.3	20.9	11.0	-3.0	-2.0	1.0	—
Services	7.6	7.8	8.0	6.4	7.0	6.6	5.8
utilities	20.6	20.3	10.0	12.0	9.8	6.6	3.0
transport/communications	7.3	6.8	7.1	6.5	6.2	4.5	5.0
commercial services	8.9	8.7	8.4	4.8	6.0	5.3	7.4
financial services	7.8	10.1	14.9	14.9	11.9	21.4	11.0
housing services	5.1	3.8	6.0	5.5	5.5	2.0	2.0
public administration	8.0	6.0	6.0	4.0	10.5	30.6	10.0
other services	5.4	7.5	8.1	8.0	7.0	-0.3	1.0
Gross domestic product	8.2	6.3	5.8	5.8	5.1	5.0	5.0

a For 1983 and 1984, components do not add to total because new constant price series for 1982–84 has been linked with old series which is in constant 1970 prices.
b Provisional.
c Includes forestry and fishing.

Table 11—*continued*

B: Balance of payments (millions of US$ at current prices)

	1978	1979	1980	1981	1982	1983	1984
Exports	950	1,135	1,297	1,346	1,305	1,360	1,755
Merchandise	846	982	1,065	1,066	1,014	1,062	1,475
Non-factor services	104	153	232	280	291	298	280
Imports	1,081	1,540	2,205	2,055	2,205	2,138	2,121
Merchandise	999	1,450	2,051	1,877	1,990	1,918	1,911
Non-factor services	82	90	154	178	215	220	210
Resource balance	−131	−405	−908	−709	−900	−778	−366
Net factor income	−15	−15	−26	−97	−98	−138	−131
factor receipts	20	40	47	33	40	43	59
factor payments	35	55	73	130	138	181	190
(interest paid)	(25)	(28)	(33)	(50)	(69)	(86)	(103)
Net current transfers	22	48	136	203	264	274	277
Transfer receipts	39	60	152	230	289	294	302
Transfer payments	17	12	16	27	25	20	25
Current balance	−124	−372	−798	−603	−734	−642	−220
Capital inflow							
Net direct investment	2	47	43	49	63	37	36
Official grant aid	58	144	138	162	162	171	154
Net loans	178	138	236	336	403	292	311
disbursements	242	187	286	380	472	373	410
repayments	64	49	50	44	69	81	99
Other (net)	0	0	0	0	0	0	0
Net short-term capital	−3	—	157	31	7	38	−26
Capital flows and other errors and omissions	−17	91	4	−8	72	105	50
Change in net reserves (− indicates increase)	−94	−48	220	33	27	−1	−305
Memo items:							
Net credit from IMF	+20	+67	−4	+165	−6	−11	+9
disbursements	48	105	39	229	43	38	32
repayments	28	38	43	64	49	49	23

and certainly is due mostly to expansion in the service sectors. Thanks to external donors, major public investments were undertaken. Along with the producer price incentives, one of these (the Mahaveli irrigation project) permitted Sri Lanka to achieve self-sufficiency in rice. Other outcomes include modest export diversification and an output profile increasingly biased towards services and away from commodity production.

Simulations with a model for Sri Lanka suggest that these outcomes might have been obtained with better distributional consequences by allocation of imports away from consumer goods and smaller public investment programmes. Mahaveli, for example, was intensive in capital and imported inputs, did not generate many jobs, and had a long lead time. However, given Bretton Woods spending priorities, it is fair to ask whether alternative, smaller scale irrigation projects could in practice have been financed.

Looking ahead, the paper's authors suggest more rational public investment, a shift back towards a dual exchange rate structure aimed at stimulating non-rice import substitution and non-traditional exports, a restoration of incomes policies like the food subsidy to aid the poor, and greater responsiveness on the part of the international agencies to the deleterious effects of the terms of trade shifts that Sri Lanka and other small, poor countries have endured.

Chile is an integral part of South America's Southern Cone, a corner of the world recently specialized in the demonstration of economic pathology. The history as told by Jose Pablo Arellano, Rene Cortazar, and Andres Solimano (1986) is a sad but illuminating chronicle of textbook orthodoxy gone fully awry. The decay is summarized in Table 12.

When the coup against the Allende government took place in 1973, triple digit inflation due to political turmoil and a redistributive, expansionary policy that had long since collided with capacity and foreign exchange limits was underway. Heavy-handed austerity got the annual rate from 600 to 37 per cent between 1974 and 1978, meanwhile doubling measured unemployment to 18 per cent at a real wage level about 30 per cent below that of 1970.[12] In June

[12] Counting people on a government works scheme, true unemployment was probably closer to 30 per cent.

Table 12　Chile: basic economic indicators

Years	Per capita GNP (1969–70 = 100)	Growth of GDP (%)	Inflation rate (%)	Unemployment rate (%)	Real wages (1969–70 = 100)	Investment rate (% GDP)	Public sector deficit (% GDP)
1970	100.0	—	36.1	5.9	100.0	20.4	2.7
1971	108.9	8.9	26.5	5.2	128.5	18.3	10.7
1972	106.4	−1.2	254.5	4.1	100.6	14.8	13.0
1973	98.3	−5.6	606.1	4.8	81.3	14.7	24.7
1974	97.1	1.0	369.2	9.1	68.1	17.4	10.5
1975	81.2	−12.9	343.3	17.6	65.9	15.4	2.6
1976	83.2	3.5	198.0	21.9	67.8	12.7	2.3
1977	90.4	9.9	84.2	18.9	74.8	13.3	1.8
1978	96.1	8.2	37.2	18.0	79.6	14.5	0.8
1979	101.8	8.3	38.9	17.3	86.1	15.6	−1.7
1980	107.5	7.8	31.2	16.9	93.5	17.6	−3.1
1981	109.8	5.7	9.5	15.1	101.9	19.5	−1.7
1982	89.8	−14.4	20.7	26.1	102.0	15.0	2.3
1983	87.8	−0.8	23.1	31.4	91.0	12.9	3.8
1984	91.2	6.3	23.0	24.0	91.2	13.6	4.0
1985	88.8	2.4	26.4	22.0	87.1	14.8	—

1979 the authorities froze the exchange rate in a final attempt to get rid of inflation via the workings of expectations and the law of one price. By mid-1982 prices were growing in the single digits but there had been 30 per cent real appreciation. Several maxi-devaluations in the second half of the year set the inflation cycle going again, at a 25 per cent inertial rate.

While all this was happening the country was hit with adverse shifts in the terms of trade which were to continue throughout the 1980s, plus the experiments in liberalization undertaken by General Pinochet's economic team.[13] In the mid-1970s enterprises nationalized under Allende were sold to several financial conglomerates closely linked with the government. Each was built around a bank. Restrictive monetary policy created high interest rates, which were further driven up by Ponzi finance and a stock market boom in which the conglomerates—blissfully unregulated by the state—borrowed from their banks to bid up their own companies' shares. Restrictions on capital inflows were weak, though there were still barriers to movements the other way. Nonetheless, foreign investors seemed willing to put money into the Chilean financial market through the widening trade deficit. Late in the decade there was an import-led boom with high levels of economic activity in non-traded sectors. An orthodox miracle seemed to be getting up steam, and was widely praised in the world financial press at the time.

The miracle was mostly the consequence of the overvalued exchange rate and the financial bubble.[14] The 1982 maxi-devaluations were forced by a current account deficit of 15 per cent of GDP, and the bubble broke in 1983 when the authorities finally had to 'intervene' with several banks (take them over). About a quarter of

[13] Why politically interventionist military dictatorships in the Southern Cone opted for extreme free market economic policies is an intriguing question. One hypothesis is that the economists involved (many trained at the University of Chicago) had a logically coherent, ideologically attractive package of policies to sell. Their emphasis on full market deregulation was consistent with 'disciplining' labour in general, and Chile's Communist party and activist middle class professional groups in particular. The fact that the theory of the 'Chicago Boys' did not fit their countries' economies did not stop them from being extremely influential all over Latin America for more than two decades.

[14] As other work by the WIDER paper's authors shows, its apparent success was abetted by the official statistical agency's underestimation of the inflation rate and overestimation of growth.

the assets of the banking system were declared to be non-performing, while the two biggest banks (each central to a conglomerate) lost more than five times their capital. Through the linkages of the banks with industrial concerns, the state ended up controlling far more of the productive apparatus than it ever had under Allende. Meanwhile, the requisite financial bail-out changed the net reserve position of the central bank (which accumulated the foreign debts of the system) from + $3 billion to − $2 billion by the end of 1985. On the side of relative prices, the 1982 devaluations ended up causing 50 per cent real depreciation. That plus austerity made GDP fall by 14 per cent, undoing most of the growth during the miracle period. A final blow came from transitory abolition of exchange controls, which set off a perfectly avoidable capital flight.

Since 1983 the government has been trying to pick up the pieces with the help of an EFF programme with the Fund and a SAL from the World Bank, each bearing its own conditionalities. Flirtation with fiscal expansion led to 6 per cent growth in 1984, but a trade deficit of 11 per cent of GDP put an end to that. Austerity and supply-side policies to try to increase output were the order of the day until copper prices surprisingly jumped upward in 1987.

The authors of the Chilean paper view the economy as a stagnationist system hovering at the edge of being foreign exchange constrained. Within Chile, regressive income redistribution has cut back demand, while two double digit recessions (in 1975 and 1982) plus stagnant investment over a decade have destroyed much capacity. The 'normal' unemployment rate as a consequence is very high. Externally, the terms of trade shocks and capital flight have brought strangulation.

Any exit from these traps must taken place over a period of years in an environment made at least predictable (forget about 'optimal' in the neoclassical sense) for a period of time. Recovery may be aided by selective trade policies, redistribution aimed at stimulating demand for local products for example, through taxes on luxury consumption instead of the tax breaks for saving that have been implemented), and renewal of the role that the Chilean state took in guiding capital formation for several decades before 1970. With respect to external relationships, debt default or forgiveness may ultimately be on the cards.

4.4 Heterodox Shocks

Liberal policy packages were tried elsewhere in South America in the 1970s, failing in ways bearing a family resemblance to what happened in Chile. In other countries—Argentina, Brazil, and Peru—the professional reaction thereafter and the restitution of democracy led to heterodox stabilization programmes based on the structuralist approach. As of writing in mid-1987, the results are not all available for these attempts. Nonetheless, enough has been learned from their successes and failures to leave some lessons for the future.

Argentina went through something of a golden age in the ten years before 1975, with trade surpluses, steady growth, and (by Southern Cone standards) moderate and stable inflation in the 30 per cent range. However, according to Roberto Frenkel, Jose Maria Fanelli, and Charlos Winograd (1987), social and economic tensions led to an inflationary burst in mid-decade while in the political arena democratic government gave way to military dictatorship. The new regime put an orthodox anti-inflationary stabilization programme into force, carrying out a sequence of liberal experiments that makes even Chile's seem tame by comparison.

Briefly, the history (summarized in figures in Table 13) goes as follows. Policies between 1976 and 1979 were orthodox traditional—austerity, devaluation, and liberalization. There was some balance of payments and growth recovery in 1977 (after the obligatory contractionary phase) but inflation was structural and did not slow. Controlling price increases became the major concern. Late in 1977 the monetary screws were tightened while controls on interest rates were let loose.[15] The real rate jumped from being slightly negative to 4.6 per cent (monthly) in the fourth quarter. Investment dropped sharply, and recession persisted into 1978. High rates pulled capital inflows through a liberalized exchange

---

[15] Such 'de-repression' of the financial system as advocated by McKinnon (1973) was in vogue at the time. The basic rationale is that if output is determined from the side of supply, then low, controlled interest rates lead to excess aggregate demand which can only be limited by an inflation tax. Increasing rates will therefore both reduce inflation and (by raising saving rates in a neoclassical long-run model) lead to faster growth.

market, weakening the central bank's control over the money supply. These outcomes of recession, faster inflation, and speculative capital movements prompted new orthodox insights into the inflationary process which were built into the policies of the subsequent phase.

The foundation for neo-monetarist stabilization was a pre-announced *tablita* of exchange rate devaluations, slowing from 5.25 per cent a month in February 1979 to zero in March 1981. Inflation was supposed to come into step, aided by public pricing and monetary supply rules tied to the 'active' exchange rate crawl. With structural inflation, the policy resoundingly failed—the devaluation and inflation rates were 63 and 160 per cent in 1979, and 24 and 101 per cent in 1980. On the financial side, slower depreciation made the return on domestic assets relative to foreign jump.[16] Capital inflows accelerated, letting imports double to 15 per cent of GDP in 1980–81. Private wealth-holders soon recognized that the illusion of external solvency could not last, and started shifting their holdings abroad. The authorities were more stubborn, and orchestrated $13 billion of foreign borrowing in 1979–80 to support their exchange rate manoeuvres. The Argentine state still owes that debt.

A period of chaotic adjustment followed: '. . . 1981 was the year of devaluation, 1982 the year of "socialization" [by an inflation tax] and "nationalization" [by a fiscal bail-out] of private liabilities, and 1983 the year of wage increases in response to strong pressure exerted by unions on a decadent military government about to give way to democracy.' A fragile, rococo financial structure emerged, embellished with special markets (a parallel exchange rate, an inter-firm market for loans, a wide open rediscount window) that the authorities perpetually struggle to keep in order.

After a year of indecision, in mid-1985 the new government imposed a heterodox anti-inflationary shock called the Austral Plan. It incorporated a wage and exchange rate freeze, together with neutral distributional and fiscal policies and creation of a new

---

[16] The point in detail is that without considering expectations of a future maxi-devaluation (which escalated over time), the returns of domestic and foreign assets will be respectively the domestic interest rate and the foreign rate plus expected depreciation. A less rapid crawling devaluation makes foreign holdings less attractive.

Table 13 Argentina: basic macroeconomic indicators

	GDP growth rate (1)	Inflation rate (CPI) (2)	Real exchange rate (3)		Real wage (4)	Balance of payments (5)		Nominal net external debt (6)
			(a)	(b)		Trade account	Current account	
1969–74	4.4	30.5	99.8	90.9	97.4	269.1	35.7	
1975–84	0.4	247.9	105.4	93.8	84.8	1166.5	−1481.5	
1970	4.5	13.6	101.6	100.5	95.5	79.1	−158.9	n.a.
1971	3.7	34.9	90.2	91.5	99.0	−127.7	−388.7	n.a.
1972	1.9	58.4	106.6	101.1	94.1	36.4	−222.9	n.a.
1973	3.4	60.3	100.0	100.0	100.0	1036.5	720.7	3948.0
1974	5.7	24.2	109.4	104.7	113.1	295.8	127.2	5359.0
1975	−0.4	182.8	112.6	88.9	105.5	−985.2	−1284.6	7256.0
1976	−0.5	444.1	142.8	110.3	71.2	883.1	649.6	6467.0
1977	6.4	176.0	119.9	110.6	71.9	1490.3	1289.9	5639.0
1978	−2.9	175.5	95.8	95.6	69.3	2565.8	1833.6	6459.0
1979	6.2	159.5	68.8	72.1	79.8	1109.9	−536.4	8554.0
1980	0.8	100.8	53.6	61.3	88.7	−2519.2	−4707.8	19478.0
1981	6.2	104.5	68.7	75.9	80.5	−287.0	−4714.0	31794.0
1982	−5.1	164.8	121.8	103.9	71.7	2286.8	−2657.7	37477.0
1983	3.1	343.8	141.1	109.5	94.5	3320.0	−2437.5	40907.0
1984	2.4	626.7	128.7	109.6	114.9	3800.0	−2190.0	44155.0

(3)a Deflator domestic prices: consumer price index (CPI)
(3)b Deflator domestic prices: wholesale industrial prices net of foodstuffs
(3) and (4) index 1973 = 100
(5) and (6) in millions of dollars

currency (the austral) in terms of which contracts were de-indexed. The package was sanctioned by the Fund, although informed sources suggest that the Argentines had to bypass the country staff to get Board approval. Up to early 1987 the Austral appeared to be a partial success, but conditions decayed thereafter.

The freeze lasted about nine months, during which supply shocks in flex-price markets produced about 2 per cent inflation per month and interest rates were kept very high. Real wage losses and cost pressures led to relaxation of the freeze, and price increases cumulated to the rate of 5 or 6 per cent per month late in 1986. Tight monetary policy towards the end of the year failed to brake the process and may have added some interest rate cost-push. A new three-month freeze (preceded by 'corrective inflation' of the exchange rate and public enterprise prices) was imposed early in 1987.

Where the freeze was lifted, inflation became vertical again, returning to levels comparable to those following the 1980 acceleration. Meanwhile, the attained reduction in inflation and real GDP growth in 1986 of about 5 per cent went hand-in-hand with a lower government deficit. Demand was supported by consumption increases which may have been caused in part by the reduction in the inflation tax that the programme produced. After years of stagnation, private investment was beginning to respond to these developments. The balance of payments was in fairly good shape (the trade surplus was not impossibly smaller than debt service obligations), and prospects for the future seemed stable if not bright. All in all, two decent years for Argentina.

Brazil's experience with a Cruzado Plan resembling the Austral was far less successful. Although the real economy was sound in early 1987, a year-long attempt at a heterodox shock had broken down and inflation was running at quadruple digit annual rates. To understand the reasons, one should recognize how past Brazilian stabilization attempts narrowed the freedom of manoeuvre in current programmes, as emphasized by Dionisio Carneiro (1987).

One major constraint from the past is a political consensus that inflation reduction should not be based on real wage cuts, as in a 1964–66 package when understatement of expected price increases combined with forward-looking wage indexation rules to worsen the income distribution. This scheme was imposed by a repressive military regime, which 15 years later was looking for a political exit more graceful than the one taken by the admirals and generals in Argentina. Not increasing inequality was viewed as one means towards that end.

A second limitation on policy came from a decision in the mid-1970s by the same government to push a massive programme of public investments (totalling billions of dollars) to assure external self-reliance by extending the import substitution process to complex intermediates and capital goods, and raising export capacity. This plan mandated a steady demand injection, and forced the state to generate a substantial flow of saving. In the late 1970s the resources should come from abroad in form of loans from commercial banks, meaning that the government and the private financial sector had to intermediate the incoming dollars into domestic capacity creation. Debt-led growth got underway in earnest after a rather orthodox stabilization based on austerity and an attempt to reduce mark-ups broke down under recession in late 1974.

A third restriction arose from the increasingly indexed nature of the Brazilian economy, not only with regard to wage increases and devaluation but also financial contracts. Interest payments on government debt were indexed to the inflation rate. This move offset the inflation tax and added little to aggregate demand, but drove the nominal public sector borrowing requirement (PSBR) sky-high. All this price and cost indexation ensured that pure demand contraction would leave inflation untouched (without wage repression as in the 1960s). Econometric results for the late 1970s and early 1980s suggested that cutting capacity utilization by 10 per cent might reduce triple digit inflation rates by ten percentage points.

These constraints could easily create an over-determined system, as began to appear after the second oil shock and the interest rate increases on foreign debt in the late 1970s. Maxi-devaluations were followed by crawling peg slow-downs on the Argentine model, predictably appreciating the exchange rate. An attempt at partial de-indexation of the financial system led to negative real interest rates. Imports flooded in, sales of durable goods soared, real estate speculation took off. After bail-out sanitation of the financial system, the stage was set for four years of orthodox stabilization—

the first two do-it-yourself followed by two more of uneasy collaboration with the IMF. Data about these stabilizations appear in Table 14.

The emphasis in the first period was on reducing absorption to improve the current account. A recession from 1981 to 1983 was the result until US growth and the coming to fruition of the investment plan dramatically improved the external situation from 1984.[17] In the IMF period, seven Letters of Intent were negotiated and then broke down over the issues of whether 100 per cent wage indexation should be cut back and the interpretation of the interest component of the PSBR. Despite austerity, inflation ratcheted up to 200 + per cent per year, and a civilian government came in. After a year of indecision (including a tax code revision which added to workers' purchasing power in the short run), it opted for the Cruzado Plan heterodox shock in February 1986.

The Cruzado failed as an anti-inflation programme because it ran into the same contradictions that had upset stabilization at the turn of the decade. The plan led with an initial 8 per cent wage increase after a price freeze to avoid a real wage cut which the government (or at least influential elements of the ruling party) felt could not be imposed. There was also a trigger clause by which real wages would automatically be restored if consumer price increases reached 20 per cent, regardless of time period. Together with the earlier tax changes the package was not distributionally neutral from the outset. It may also not have been fiscally neutral, though given the state of Brazilian public accounts the case is hard to make either way.[18] Certainly there was fairly loose monetary policy in the first months of the plan, as low real interest rates prevailed.

The economy went into a boom, as redistribution and fiscal demand acted together with changes in behavioural relationships that the programme surely created (lower inflation tax, Fisher

[17] Internal relative price shifts, e.g. increases for energy products, helped along the process on the side of import substitution. Two maxi-devaluations, in 1979 and 1983, generated short-run export response.

[18] The increasing financial manipulations of the state (plus a degree of deviousness on the part of those making policy) produced a bewildering array of central and state government, public enterprise, and monetary budgets in the 1970s. Coupled with uncertainty about the effects of indexation, the inconsistent, incomplete budgets make quantification of the true fiscal position of the state a Brazilian version of the Holy Grail.

Table 14 Brazil: macroeconomic indicators and external accounts

A: Growth, inflation, real wages, monetary and fiscal data (1979–85)

	1979	1980	1981	1982	1983	1984	1985
GDP (1)	7.2	9.1	−3.4	0.9	−2.5	5.7	8.3
Industrial output (1)	6.9	9.2	−10.2	−0.2	−5.5	7.0	8.5
Inflation (2)	77.2	110.2	95.2	99.7	211.0	223.8	235.1
Agricultural prices (2)	80.5	138.2	70.7	89.5	335.8	230.5	267.7
Industrial prices (2)	78.8	110.3	99.6	99.8	200.5	233.2	221.1
Industrial real wages (3)	100.0	96.0	100.1	109.9	94.5	87.3	93.4
Monetary base (1)	2.9	−15.0	−22.9	−5.4	−23.0	−20.4	2.1
Money supply (1)	−0.8	−12.2	−21.0	−6.5	−27.7	−24.4	7.9
Financial assets (1)	1.9	−13.2	−2.2	24.8	0.1	1.2	20.3
Loans to private sector (1)	2.1	−12.5	−11.3	7.7	−6.5	−12.3	3.8
Loans from monetary authorities (1)	−4.5	−11.8	−24.9	−15.3	−26.9	−37.6	−3.5
PSBR/GDP (4)	4.9	4.3	5.8	7.1	7.5	9.3	—
Adjusted deficit/GDP (4)	3.0	1.9	3.2	3.1	0.1	2.2	—
Average nominal interest rates (5)	41.2	38.3	90.7	115.7	170.1	245.3	248.2

(1) Real rates of growth
(2) December to December
(3) Deflated by the General Prices Index (IGP-DI), 1979 = 100
(4) Author's estimates
(5) Short-term (91 days) government bills (LTH's), annual averages

Table 14—*continued*

B: selected data on external accounts (1979–85)

	1979	1980	1981	1982	1983	1984	1985
Exports (US$ billion)	15.2	20.1	23.3	20.4	21.9	27.0	25.6
% GDP	6.7	8.4	8.7	7.6	10.7	12.8	11.6
Imports (US$ billion)	18.1	22.9	22.1	19.6	15.4	13.9	13.2
% GDP	8.0	9.5	8.3	7.3	7.5	6.6	6.0
Trade balance (US$ billion)	−2.8	−2.8	1.2	0.8	6.5	13.1	12.4
Terms of trade (1977=100)							
total	79	65	55	54	53	58	58
non-oil	81	78	71	69	64	71	79
Growth of world imports (%)	5.4	1.0	0.7	−0.3	1.4	9.0	3.0
Net exports (goods and services)							
US$ billion	−5.2	−5.9	−1.6	−2.8	4.1	11.4	10.5
% GDP	−2.3	−2.5	−0.6	−1.0	2.0	5.4	4.7
Interest payments (US$ billion)	4.2	6.3	9.2	11.4	9.6	10.1	10.4
% exports	27.5	31.3	39.3	56.8	43.6	37.3	40.6
Interest rates (average)	13.2	15.7	19.5	21.1	14.6	13.3	12.7
Net debt/exports	2.6	2.3	2.3	3.3	3.5	3.0	3.1
Real exchange rate (1977=100)	88.8	87.3	79.8	72.7	91.9	90.9	93.6

effects of unknown strength and magnitude, and so on). Flex-prices began to rise, not just for food but (as in Argentina) also clothes at the retail level. In markets for meat and similar products, suppliers held stocks back in anticipation of future inflation—a manoeuvre made easier by low real interest rates. There were real estate and stock market flurries. Finally, some prices (for cars, for example) had been pegged artificially low, but the government did not take the occasion of decreases in the overall index in the first months of the plan to make corrections. Low mark-up rates (despite high capacity use) increased distributional unrest on the part of the entrepreneurial sector.

Finally, the political and economic cycles went in opposite directions. There were timid steps toward demand restraint in July, but national elections were schedule for November and nothing further was done. Imports soared and exports declined by October—the unfortunately named 'Cruzado II' package announced just after government victories in the election was stillborn. The combined effects of capacity and foreign exchange restrictions turned a stagnationist economy into one where forced saving inflationary adjustments, abetted by the wage trigger, ruled. By early 1987 four-digit annual inflation rates began to appear. The response in June (by a new Finance Minister) was a three-month wage and price freeze coupled with a maxi-devaluation and austerity; the obvious danger is that such a package will degenerate into partial de-indexation and stop–go policies like those pursued earlier in the decade. The saving grace, perhaps, is that thanks to the state's heterodox investment programme prospects on the trade account are favourable. Debt relief or repudiation may create enough appropriable economic surplus for another serious anti-inflation attempt which will not break out of the socially acceptable range of distribution manoeuvre.

Peru arrived at heterodoxy with an Inti Plan in 1985 after a long and painful journey through political fluctuation, external shocks, and orthodox remedies jointly applied by Bretton Woods and local economists. According to Richard Webb (1987) the economy has gone through two major cycles since the early 1970s. Political factors led into the first. A populist military regime changed the rules of the game brusquely. Poorly administered land reform and laws for the gradual redistribution of industrial and mining properties to workers provoked capital flight. By mid-decade stagflation was added to legal uncertainty. Price increases accelerated as the economy swung towards forced saving adjustment with distributional conflict. The favourable export circumstances of the previous quarter century deteriorated with world prices and trade volumes becoming unstable. Output stagnated, and investment dropped off.

There was an externally-based recovery in 1979–80, associated with, but not principally caused by, an orthodox stabilization package. Higher foreign exchange inflows came from favourable shifts in external prices, a big new copper mine, and an oil pipeline over the Andes, *plus* healthy growth in non-traditional exports. Increased oil supplies also permitted imports to be cut. The non-traditional exports were the positive outcome of the stabilization, stimulated by devaluation and an absorption cut. Less favourable aspects of the programme included stagnant agriculture (the land reform had diverted attention from public investment and productivity in the sector), low investment, and stable export volumes after the capacity jump. Inflation, which had accelerated to 60–70 per cent per year from its traditional 10 per cent, was attacked with import liberalization and tight money. As protection declined and the exchange rate appreciated at the turn of the decade, the manufacturing sector went flat. Price increases at best slowed marginally.

Despite these structural weaknesses, a new government's policy team entered the 1980s with faith in fiscal discipline and liberalization as keys to success. The case studies for Chile and Argentina already document how such ideas were in the Latin air at the time. As in the other countries, they were soon to be sorely stressed in Peru.

A major crisis played through 1982–83, with GDP falling 16 per cent in 15 months and inflation accelerating to 120 per cent. These disastrous numbers resulted from a confluence of orthodox policies in 1981–82, natural disasters early in 1983, and an inability of policy-makers to comprehend how difficult the situation really was because of their theoretical preconceptions and lack of information.

Some combination (with weights uncertain) of tight money and liberalization fed into stagflation in 1982. Price increases ran faster, though in October the Fund staff still viewed 'tightening of fiscal and monetary policy . . . as a critical factor in bringing about a substantial reduction of inflation in 1983'. Meanwhile, the external situation—export prices, interest rates, access to credit—turned at least as sour for Peru as for the rest of the developing world. Beginning in December, six months of torrential rains followed by drought hit the country as a consequence of an unprecedented surge in 'El Nino', the famous Southern Pacific climatic instability which also had a hand in contemporaneous African drought. These external shocks are roughly quantified in Table 15.

Table 15   Peru: balance of payments shocks, 1983–85 ($ millions)

	1983	1985	Change
Exogenous items			
Exports	3015	2966	−49
terms of trade effect			−410
El Nino effect			500
other			−139
Net disbursements of long-term credits to public sector	385	−671	−1056
Registered net private long- and short-term credits	−810	−307	503
Services and other items	−1165	−1031	134
Errors and omissions	211	−220	−431
Balancing items			−899
Imports [increase(−)]	2722	1869	853
Refinancing	1024	1450	426
Change in reserves [increase (−)]	−40	318	−380

A dialogue of the deaf ensued between the Bretton Woods agencies and the Peruvian authorities. As late as April 1984 an IMF press release claimed that the '. . . major factor behind the imbalances in the Peruvian economy during 1982 and 1983 was the large deficit of the non-financial public sector'. Although they dominated headlines at that time, El Nino and a 35 per cent fall in export prices between 1980 and 1984 were mentioned but not given much significance in the release.

On the part of the Peruvians, the first half of 1983 was devoted to absorbing the gravity of the situation: in conversation Webb observes that an earthquake would have been far easier to grasp than a climatic shock which gradually washed out 5 per cent of GDP. It was important to maintain confidence (if only because 40 per cent of the money supply was in dollar-denominated deposits); as a consequence the government and the Bretton Woods staff played charades. In March 1983, '. . . GDP was projected to grow 0.9%, exports 8.8%, and prices 55% that year. The actual rates in 1983 were -12.3% in GDP, -8% in exports, and 111% inflation. Tax revenue was projected to drop 6%; in fact it fell 31%.'

Later that year, local commonsense rebelled. Holding down state enterprise prices and the exchange rate slowed inflation to 63 per cent at an annual rate from the side of costs, while easy credit was utilized for disaster relief as well as to support firms' balance sheets. In 1984 policy turned inconsistent. The Architect-President Fernando Belaunde Terry wanted dollars to complete his investment projects, the Industry Minister turned unorthodox in imposing import controls to protect local activity, two successive Finance Ministers waxed expansionary and contractionary in turn, and the Central Bank rediscovered high interest rates to defend against capital flight. Fiscal expansion and import controls led respectively to disagreements with the Fund and World Bank. More or less unwittingly, the government stopped meeting external interest payments in August; by design the election campaign in late 1984 was used to disguise real depreciation and fiscal deficit cuts.

President Alan Garcia's government took office in mid-1985. A heterodox shock Inti Plan reduced inflation to less than 100 per cent. No targets for slower prices were set out, though the government has been happy to take credit for favourable results. Second, the new programme is oriented towards redistribution, in part by shifting the terms of trade towards agricultural producers (itself an inflationary move). Peru's economy is stagnationist, so demand and growth in 1985–86 were high. Obvious questions are how soon capacity and/or foreign exchange limits will be reached, and whether *dirigiste* policy will bring decreasing efficiency returns. With regard to potential constraints, the shift in the terms of trade may stimulate food production while the previous regime's departing devaluation and *de facto* repudiation of external interest payments (made an explicit policy by the new government) opened space on the foreign exchange front. As of mid-1987, the economy seemed to be lapsing into an output-constrained, forced saving adjustment mode. Time and the Garcia team's canniness will tell how successfully this tendency will be overcome.

4.5 Two Special Cases

We close with India and South Korea, two economies different from each other and those discussed before them. Each has its own sectoral growth and price formation style, posing unique problems for macro policy in the short run.

India has twice tried stabilizing external shocks. The first programme involved a devaluation-cum-liberalization in 1966 aimed to please external aid donors after disagreements with China and Pakistan broke into wars; the second was an orthodox package following the first oil shock in 1973. Both seemed successful, but not for the usual reasons. Their outcomes illustrate the shifting constraints under which Indian macroeconomic policy must be designed. Table 16 and Figures 3A and 3B illustrate the trade-offs involved.

Table 16   India: composition of aggregate demand

	Govt. Cons.	Public Inv.	Private Cons.	Private Inv.	$C+C$	$I_p + I_c$
1970–71	9.3	6.8	72.8	11.2	82.1	17.9
1971–72	3.9	7.0	71.4	11.7	81.3	18.7
1972–73	9.8	7.4	72.6	10.2	82.4	17.6
1973–74	8.6	8.1	72.3	11.0	80.3	19.1
1974–75	8.5	7.8	71.5	12.2	80.0	20.0
1975–76	9.6	10.0	68.9	11.4	78.5	21.5
1976–77	10.3	10.7	67.6	11.4	77.9	22.1
1977–78	9.7	8.3	69.7	12.3	79.4	20.6
1978–79	9.6	9.7	67.4	13.3	77.0	23.0
1979–80	9.9	10.7	66.4	13.0	76.3	23.7
1980–81	9.8	10.5	66.6	13.1	76.4	23.6
1981–82	9.9	11.4	66.1	12.6	76.0	24.0

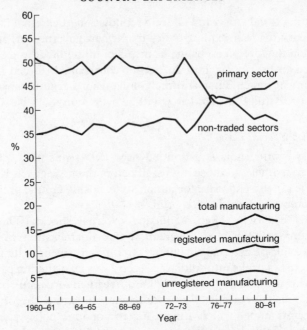

Fig. 3A   India: sectoral gross product shares in GDP

Pronab Sen (1987) argues that growth in the Indian economy is potentially constrained by one of three factors: potential saving, food supply, or available foreign exchange. Drawing on a model constructed by Abhijit Sen (1981) he argues that prior to the early 1970s available foreign exchange would have permitted faster growth than potential saving, and saving faster growth than food supply. The observed GDP growth rate of 2.9 per cent was just under the agricultural limit.

Around the beginning of the last decade the story began to change. Trend agricultural output growth accelerated (due to new technology, public investment in irrigation, and supportive price policy), although the economy remained vulnerable to adverse food supply shocks from bad monsoons. At the same time the income distribution shifted towards the urban middle classes for several reasons (worsening agricultural terms of trade, a falling wage share), making the aggregate consumption basket more intensive in imports and less in food. Investment rose, absorbing increased

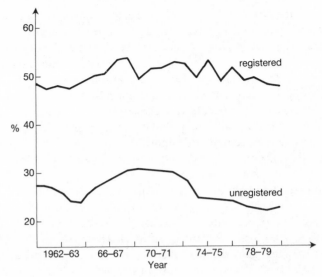

Fig. 3B India: wage share in manufacturing sectors

saving from income concentration and also drawing in imports. With the rise in oil prices, all these shifts made foreign exchange the binding restriction on growth. The constraint change, however, did not become apparent until after the second oil shock because India had access to low conditionality IMF finance (first tranche drawings and the Oil Facilities) plus foreign aid, as well as gowing commodity export and labour remittance inflows from the Middle East).

Against this background, we can consider the stabilization episodes. The 1966 devaluation has been widely discussed—it symbolized the end of Jawaharlal Nehru's era of independent, planned economic growth. The exchange rate revision was tied to transitory removal of export subsidies and import liberalization, giving roughly 43 per cent real depreciation for imports and 22 per cent for exports. It was followed by expansionary fiscal and monetary policy, with 15 per cent inflation and stable real interest rates. Also, export incentives and import quotas were rapidly reinstalled. Growth accelerated and the trade balance improved. Why did these favourable outcomes occur?

Sen points to several reasons. First, the marginal propensity to consume rose substantially in 1966–67, due to reduced national saving in the face of a major crop failure. Run-downs of food stocks, increased state transfer payments, and a shift in the terms of trade towards the low saving agricultural sector were involved. The upward shift in the consumption function offset the contractionary effects of the devaluation. Later, expansionary macro policy, a degree of price responsiveness in the import basket, renewed export incentives, and an agricultural recovery permitted growth to be sustained. Despite all the publicity it has received, the 1966 devaluation represented little more than a blip in the country's economic trajectory.

The constraint shift in the early 1970s was more profound. It was accompanied by tight monetary and fiscal policy after the oil shock, with real interest rates rising to 15 per cent while public investment was cut. There was effective exchange rate depreciation, due to India's sterling peg. The outcomes in the latter part of the decade included stable growth, low inflation, and a good current account performance. One important cause was the outstanding agricultural performance, which by itself would have permitted 6 instead of 4 per cent annual GDP increases without food demand inflation. Instead, 30 million ton stocks of food grains (several months' supply) were built up and the terms of trade fell, restraining price increases overall. Stabilization was also helped by the favourable external factors mentioned above. The upshot was that output was effectively held down by control over demand. With hindsight one can say that the contractionary stabilization moves just cut consumption without adding to potential growth.

Looking into the future, policy must operate under several limitations implicit in the Indian system. Payment rules for the middle classes (labour in 'organized' manufacturing and pro-prietors and the salariat in the expanding non-traded sector) begin to cut their real income flows when inflation runs faster than about 6 per cent. The political power of these groups plus a staunch national belief in monetarist inflation theory help explain a deflationary bias in macro policy. At the same time, shifts in the key relative price— the agricultural terms of trade—can only be achieved through inflation, given downward wage rigidity. Sen suggests that in the absence of supply shocks from bad harvests, keeping the terms of trade stable provides a guideline for fiscal policy since agricultural prices respond sensitively to changes in aggregate demand.

A degree of inflation will result from this rule (which should also be adjusted to keep growth within foreign exchange bounds). Resulting real appreciation should be offset by a crawling multiple-rate exchange structure, with a depreciated 'key' rate for price-sensitive exports and non-intermediate imports. Intermediate imports and capital movements could be regulated with subsidiary rates. With a bad harvest, for example, the intermediate import rate could be appreciated to cut inflation and the private capital rate depreciated to bring in foreign exchange (assuming that excessive leakage between markets can be avoided). Imports should be further governed with quotas, along lines now well-established in bureaucratic protocol.

The central thrust of these recommendations is towards a stable policy course, trying to keep the growth rate as close to constrained limits as possible without triggering forced saving adjustment processes in India's complex social milieu. Sen argues that any incipient inflation signalling attempts at redistribution would run foul of the overwhelming political power of the middle classes. Since the rich and near-rich (say the top 5 or 10 per cent of households in the income distribution) can protect themselves against economic shocks, the poor are left vulnerable to distributional shifts. Such tensions explain why distribution-sensitive economic variables (inflation, the internal terms of trade, saving–consumption ratios, import and/or luxury intensity of the consumption basket) are watched closely in India. Since a change in the status quo could presage a cumulative process which would irreversibly harm some economic group, the state's room for manoeuvre in formulating economic policy is limited. In such circumstances, whether the famous 'Hindu rate of growth' of 3 + per cent per year can be accelerated is a difficult question for stabilization and medium term planning in future years.

South Korea is the industrial miracle of the second half of the twentieth century, passing from a 'basket case' just after the peninsular war ended in 1953 to an equal competitor with Japan and the United States in the 1980s. Korean industrialization intertwined with its stabilization episodes, and strongly conditioned both the policies applied and their results. Table 17 gives a minimal statistical picture of these events.

Alice Amsden (1987) begins her review of Korean experience

Table 17 South Korea: basic macroeconomic indicators

Year	GNP growth rate	Change in GNP deflator	Export growth rate[a]	Export growth rate[b]	Real effective exchange rate[c]	Ratio of current account to GNP	Terms of trade[c]
1962	2.2	13.5	31.7	31.0	112.0	-2.0	n.a.
1963	9.1	28.3	61.1	61.6	134.4	-3.7	111.3
1964	9.6	30.0	37.9	37.6	106.3	-0.8	112.5
1965	5.8	6.3	45.8	43.0	91.6	0.3	114.3
1966	12.7	14.2	42.9	38.3	96.1	-2.7	127.7
1967	6.6	15.8	34.0	33.7	107.9	-4.1	132.2
1968	11.3	15.9	45.1	41.5	115.2	-7.4	137.7
1969	13.8	14.6	35.4	30.3	120.1	-7.3	132.6
1970	7.6	15.7	34.0	29.3	124.2	-7.1	133.8
1971	8.8	13.4	28.5	24.3	120.7	-8.7	132.7
1972	5.7	16.4	47.9	41.7	109.4	-3.5	132.1
1973	14.1	13.4	95.9	73.2	92.4	-2.3	125.4
1974	7.7	29.5	37.5	15.7	93.6	-10.9	102.1
1975	6.9	25.8	10.8	1.4	93.5	-9.0	92.1
1976	14.1	20.5	56.2	49.2	103.4	-1.1	105.1
1977	12.7	15.8	28.6	21.1	103.9	0.0	112.4
1978	9.7	21.9	26.5	17.4	101.0	-2.2	117.8
1979	6.5	21.1	15.7	2.8	110.7	-6.4	115.3
1980	-5.2	25.6	17.1	2.6	100.0	-8.7	100.0
1981	6.2	15.9	20.1	10.0	103.1	-6.9	97.9
1982	5.6	7.1	1.0	-1.0	106.9	-3.7	102.2
1983	9.5	3.0	11.1	9.8	100.2	-2.1	103.1
1984	7.6	4.0	13.5	10.9	97.8	-1.7	105.3

[a] Growth rate in nominal US$.
[b] Export value deflated by US WPI.
[c] 1980=100.

with the coup that put President Park Chung Hee in power in 1962. During the 1950s South Korea had already taken advantage of foreign aid and market access granted by the United States to stabilize inflation and move into low wage textile production. However, there was stagnation late in the decade, and the Park regime moved decisively towards industrial growth backed by a massive educational effort and emphasis on the accumulation of capital and technical know-how. The road chosen was through exports. Foreign sales targets were set on a firm-by-firm basis and ample credit was given to exporting firms. They were also given duty-free access to intermediate imports, while industries targeted for development had tariff protection. Aside from cars (where a twenty-year development cycle was permitted), protected industries were pressed to begin exporting at once. If targets were not met, withholding credit (plus other, less delicate pressures) provided a basis for coercion. The export targets allowed planners to monitor and control the outcomes of their subsidies directly—an effective feedback control mechanism in a highly centralized state.

Foreign borrowing also played a key role in the strategy. It was used in the long run to finance investment and in the short to bring in external resources to offset external crises. Borrowing rose substantially after 1965 when deposit and interest rates were doubled at banking institutions. Firms went abroad to finance their capital formation, and the foreign debt/GDP ratio rose from 6.8 per cent in 1965 to 13.6 per cent in 1967. The GDP share of investment doubled (from 15 to 30 per cent) between 1965 and 1969, with the counterpart saving increase coming from the trade deficit, central government, and households in that order.[19]

The first stabilization episode was set off in 1970–71. Late in the 1960s the government began to rein in debt accumulation at the behest of the IMF. Export expansion slowed (from 36 to 'only' 27 per cent per year), and GDP growth was down to 7.6 per cent in

[19] The Korean interest rate reform is the centrepiece of the de-repressionist argument for liberalizing financial markets. As in Latin America, results from the reform mostly show that increasing local rates can draw capital in. Channelling the inflow to investment and keeping it from leaving via capital flight were the key to success in Korea (and also Brazil in the 1970s). The key was put in the lock by hands-on planning, generous industrial price incentives, and exchange controls, not markets.

1970. There was a 12 per cent devaluation in 1971, which raised the won cost of debt financing. The state responded with a decree in August 1972 writing down the values of loads firms had taken on the curb market and reducing bank interest rates to stimulate investment demand.

The 1971–72 exercise set a pattern for later stabilizations: a maxi-devaluation, a cut in interest rates, and a bail-out of financially troubled firms. Price controls were brought into play in 1972 (in emulation of US President Nixon's experiment the year before) to break an inflation triggered by the maxi. They remained on the books for future application. Finally, two differences with later policy should be noted. First, the initial real depreciation persisted into 1973; subsequent maxis were rapidly appreciated away. Second, there was no major recourse to foreign borrowing, in contrast to what happened in 1974–75 and at the end of the decade.

By 1973 the economy was booming again. There was also a major change in planning strategy, as the government pushed into heavy industry—steel, shipbuilding, cement—in partnership with the major economic groups or *chaebol*. The first oil shock led to a characteristic stabilization response. A decision was taken to fully pass the energy cost increase into local prices. Domestic credit was allowed to expand 40 per cent to offset the rise in the cost of production. The external deficit in an energy-dependent economy was financed by reserve depletion (-3.5 per cent of GDP in one year) and borrowing. Total foreign debt rose by 42 per cent between 1973 and 1974. The real exchange rate was kept in line (but not depreciated) by a maxi-devaluation of 22 per cent at the end of 1974. Price controls were deployed to hold inflation in the 30 per cent range.

In 1975 export growth fell to 1.4 per cent as the world economy contracted. However, capital goods imports were held back by controls, and the current account deficit fell from 11 to 9 per cent of GDP. Exports and growth took off again in 1976. But even during the preceding two years aggressive internal macro policy and borrowing kept output growth rates in the 7 per cent range—austerity was distinctly not the rule.

Inflation began to pick up in the late 1970s, spurred from the cost side by agricultural prices and (especially) wage increases. Some observers saw a 'turning point' in Korea's economic history, with an unlimited supply of agricultural labour coming to an end.[20] At the same time, the heavy industry programme began to come on stream, laying the basis for sustained export growth in the 1980s. The political consensus began to unravel, leading to the assassination of Park Chung Hee in October 1979 and his replacement as strongman after a lapse of eight months by Chun Doo Whan. The earlier push towards industrialization at all costs ceased to be the ruling economic ideology, and a 'Comprehensive Stabilization Plan' (CSP) put together by American-trained technicians was announced in 1979. It had two components: structural change to be pursued along liberal lines, and policies aimed at offsetting the second oil price shock. The latter moves were familiar, aimed at 'driving away the domestic blues with expansionary measures'.

After some initial dabbling with tight money, interest rates were reduced and credit expanded by 1981. A major scandal erupted on the curb market in 1982, prompting the creation of even more credit in the bail-out operation. A 17 per cent devaluation in 1980 was followed by a managed float—the modest real depreciation had eroded by 1983. By that time export growth pulled the economy around. Imports had risen sharply in the late 1970s due to the oil price increase and bad harvests, but thereafter stayed roughly in line with GDP growth. Higher external interest rates hurt the service account, but the cost items were offset by borrowing. The ratio of total debt to GDP rose from 32 per cent in 1979 (the last year of the industrial Big Push) to 48 per cent in 1981. As in the previous stabilizations, investment was kept up (to just under 30 per cent of GDP) by easy money and direct state action. The growth rate went 5 per cent negative in 1980, but picked eleven points back up in the following year.

A final success was inflation reduction, aided by very high productivity increases (in the order of 10 per cent per year) and price controls. This successful, underplayed heterodox shock was set in concrete by relatively tight monetary and fiscal policy beginning in 1983, plus the absence of effective wage indexation rules.

In the future, the CSP is aimed at reshaping the economy along

[20] One might note that farmer interests had been zealously protected during the industrial push. There was a land reform in 1949, and consumer food prices were kept high on the Japanese model to maintain the rural income position.

liberal lines: abolition of the export credit scheme, reduction of subsidies to farmers, plus import liberalization still wrapped in ample strands of red tape. However, the *chaebol* remain entrenched as industrial oligopolies and small and medium firms are not flourishing. Politics responds to student pressures for democratization, which have intensified over time. In Amsden's view, 'democracy may prove the only method to insure that the diversified business groups remain productive while serving the workforce at large and the public interest'. Liberal economic policy will be largely irrelevant to this issue, just as it was to industrialization and stabilization in the previous phase.

4.6 A Scorecard on Stabilizations

Summarizing the vignettes just presented is out of the question. What one can do, perhaps, is ask if different sorts of policies can effectively guide an economy towards the goals mentioned in Chapter 2—high output and growth, slow inflation, external self-reliance, and desired changes in the income distribution. We begin by reviewing the effects of policies usually considered orthodox—fiscal austerity, monetary tightness (interpreted as high interest rates), devaluation, trade and exchange liberalization, and income policies—and then go on to alternatives that are mentioned in the WIDER studies. Each policy, needless to say, acts on all the goals just mentioned: the economy is a seamless web. In a brief review, all that can be done is point out the linkages emphasized by the authors of the country papers.

Fiscal austerity can be directed towards various goals, notably increasing the trade surplus and slowing inflation. It typically acts by reducing the level of economic activity, with Ghana in the recent period being the only WIDER example of an economy with a good growth record in the face of policies aimed at restraining aggregate demand. Trade balance improvement from import cuts caused by lower output and/or investment was emphasized by paper authors for Nicaragua (under the Somozas), Ivory Coast, Tanzania, Mexico, Philippines, Sri Lanka, Colombia, Brazil, and Chile. Higher exports associated with a reduction in domestic absorption are mentioned for the more industrial countries in the preceding list, plus Turkey. In all cases, quantity adjustment stands out. As discussed in Chapters 2 and 3, orthodox theory about improving the trade balance rests upon substitution responses to relative price shifts between traded and non-traded goods which austerity is supposed to induce. Such effects do not often appear important in the short run, although some country authors (e.g. Colombia, India) indicate that they may matter over longer periods of time.

In fighting inflation, austerity's successes are not frequent: Ghana, the Philippines, and India are the more favourable cases. All are characterized by flex-price rules for a large share of final products and no great degree of cost indexation (of either wages or the exchange rate). Failures—constant or increasing inflation rates while fiscal deficits were being cut—occurred at various times in most of the Latin countries, South Korea, and Tanzania. One might also add that austerity was associated with deterioration of the income distribution in several economies, notably Sri Lanka and Mexico. By cutting public and private investment, contractionary policy reduced prospects for long-run self-reliance in Mexico and elsewhere.

Tight monetary policy goes together with fiscal austerity in most countries in the sample, since domestic capital markets do not permit open market operations or similar moves. If in addition high interest rates are imposed, they lead to output contraction in most cases. The cost-push link of higher rates to faster inflation is mentioned for the Ivory Coast, Philippines, and Turkey.

Devaluation can help the trade balance by causing either output contraction or expenditure and production substitution. Its activity-reducing role is mentioned for Mexico, the Philippines, and other countries. Favourable but often minor substitution responses (including smuggled goods clawed back into the official domain) are mentioned for Ghana, Tanzania, Sri Lanka, Brazil, Colombia (in the long run), India, and South Korea. In most of these cases the authors emphasize that the apparent response of trade flows to price incentives would not have taken place in the absence of prior or concurrent public interventions such as investment programmes. Substitution is deemed weak or perverse in Kenya, Philippines, Mexico, Egypt, and Chile. On the capital account, a weak exchange rate may draw capital inflows or slow flight, possibilities mentioned but not given great significance in several country studies.

Liberalization is supposed to improve efficiency and cut inflation. The former effect is stressed in none of the studies and denied emphatically in some, for example Mexico. Tanzania, Ghana, and Sri Lanka saw combinations of slower price increases, higher imports, and domestic de-industrialization as consequences of trade liberalization. In the Southern Cone and elsewhere exchange liberalization paved the way for capital flight. Tight exchange controls—a heterodox policy—helped keep capital from leaving Brazil, Colombia, and South Korea.

Finally, what of the claim that policy orthodoxy unlocks capital inflows? If any coherent policy package is tied with generous balance of payments support, its outcomes are likely to look better—Tanzania and Ghana (both recently), Sri Lanka, South Korea, and Turkey are cases in point. On the other hand, Colombia, Peru, and Argentina have had some heterodox success without major capital infusions while Kenya, Tanzania, and the Ivory Coast all tried to play by the rules early in the 1980s but had support cut off. Mexico, Egypt, and the Philippines at various times were orthodox failures well supported by commercial banks and the Bretton Woods agencies. The implication is that causal connections among policy lines, external support, and final outcomes are tangled and complex.

Turning to non-orthodox approaches, the good medium-term growth records based on expansionary policy in South Korea and Brazil stand out. Public investment, export subsidies, easy credit, and exchange and import controls all played a role in these success cases. Import controls also proved helpful in Nicaragua, Colombia, Kenya, India, and elsewhere. Besides South Korea and Brazil, export subsidies have paid off in Turkey, India, and Colombia. Finally, the success ratio on heterodox shock anti-inflation policies is about even—Argentina for a time, Peru, and (in an offhand way) South Korea are partial successes; Brazil is a failure.

In closing, one might wonder if certain policies are more appropriate to some types of countries than others. No general rules of thumb emerge beyond the rather detailed linkages spelled out in Table 1. Much depends on current institutional and political circumstances in the economy at hand. Indeed, that should be the main lesson from the country studies. Tolstoy began *Anna Karenina* with the observation that 'All happy families are alike, but each unhappy family is unhappy in its own special way'. If for 'family' we read 'stabilization', the epigraph surely applies to the unhappy cases. Unfortunately it fails for the happy ones, which are also unique in their own ways. Therein lies the art of economic policy in the short run.

5

How Stabilization Can Be Made to Work Better

So far, we have seen how similar IMF/World Bank stabilization packages generate a spectrum of results when applied in the historically diverse circumstances of the Third World. 'Success' and 'failure' in stabilization are relative notions, but a fair assessment would say that the outcomes of orthodox packages ranged from moderately successful to disastrous. Fewer heterodox programmes have been tried. They avoided endings as painful as those in the Southern Cone and Mexico, but produced no famous victories. Is there any way we can use economic reasoning to sort out why policies went wrong or right? More generally, do the WIDER country studies suggest approaches to stabilization better balanced than the standard, avoiding output contraction, regressive redistribution, and financial collapse?

In this chapter these questions are approached from several angles. First, Chapter 4's country histories and the theory in Chapters 2 and 3 suggest that both grand forces and specific linkages determine how macroeconomics works in developing economies. The world is complicated—Table 1 in Chapter 3 gives detail in ample amounts. A convenient way to summarize it is in terms of thesis/antithesis pairs. Section 5.1 is devoted to 15 such contrasts. At least at the level of rhetoric, the Fund and Bank predictably favour their market-oriented sides. Their line on macroeconomics constitutes a very special case. The probabalistically minded will observe that it boils down to one in 2^{15} or 32,768 ways of looking at the world.

How this theory is reflected in the IMF's 'financial programming' exercises is the topic of Section 5.2, followed in Section 5.3 with suggestions for extending this formal methodology to deal with developing countries as they are. Section 5.4 takes up less abstract aspects of stabilization. One is a recent UNICEF proposal for adjustment 'with a human face', which could conceivably fit into Bretton Woods programmes. Recent changes in Bank/Fund rhetoric and practice are then reviewed: they are perhaps more favourable to policy along the lines suggested by WIDER authors than official pronouncements would suggest. Finally, contrasts between market-oriented and planned development strategies lead in Section 5.5 to considerations about how successful transitions from stabilization to medium-term growth might in practice be attained.

5.1 Theses on Bretton Woods

The theses in the following discussion are attributed to mainstream economics and the institutions from Bretton Woods; the truth is not greatly distorted thereby.[1] The antitheses are structuralist in orientation. Practical syntheses about macroeconomics in the Third World have yet to appear. Effectively, this essay is devoted to informed guesses about the form they may take.

The contrasts first deal with grand lines of macroeconomic adjustment—the nature of inflation, the relative importance of fix-price and flex-price markets, whether forced saving or output adjustment rules and (if the latter) whether the economy is stagnationist or exhilarationist—and then illustrate how specific balance of payments and financial linkages determine the results of different policy moves. They go as follows:

1. Inflation can be set off by monetarist or structuralist forces. The simplest monetarist theory says that money creation is a good proxy for excess demand in the economy, and that prices rise more or less proportionately to the growth of money supply. Structural theories are built on inflationary shocks and propagation mechanisms. A shock can come from excess demand or changes in the income distribution—examples of the latter are real wage losses from higher food prices or reduced national purchasing power due to a jump in import costs (for example from devaluation). A decline

---

[1] On the other hand, argument by disjunction does tend towards oversimplification. In the present context, the main danger lies in drawing caricatures of the Bank and Fund. In particular, individual staff members of these institutions (and the policies they at times propose) are not in accord with the views attributed to their employers. They deserve an apology for being judged guilty by association, and a pat on the back for having independent minds. Socializing pressures are fierce along both sides of 19th Street in Washington DC.

in the real income of any economically powerful group creates potential for inflation. In self-defence the group will force up nominal prices over which it has some control. These increases can drive up prices influenced by other groups. Such feedback loops propagate an inflationary process. At the extreme, inflation becomes inertial if 'most' micro prices are indexed to their economy-wide average rate of growth. In structural inflations, money supply and/or velocity accommodate to price increases built into all contracts in the system.

The WIDER country experiences suggest that one or the other of these theories applies better, depending on the circumstances. In a specific context, some blend of the two (since neither is a full explanation of inflation) makes sense. The IMF view would be that monetarism and not structuralism is correct. Corollaries are that money supply and velocity are predetermined in the short run, the former to a large extent by government deficit spending. Velocity to a first approximation is constant; to a second it rises as a function of the inflation rate.

2. Inflation better approximates the monetarist model if most markets in the economy are price-clearing (the usual examples are food products and services) and indexation of nominal payments is not widespread. Mark-up or administered pricing plus indexation support inflations along structuralist lines. Specific markets may change their pricing rules. An example is the proliferation of parallel transactions and urban subsistence activities in Africa over the past ten years.

The Fund view is that most markets have flexible prices: mark-ups and indexation are epiphenomena to excess money creation when there is inflation. Especially in Latin America, WIDER authors would be opposed.

3. The mode of macroeconomic adjustment matters for both output and price determination. If output (perhaps disaggregated by institutionally relevant sectors) is close to the upper bounds imposed by capacity or available foreign exchange, then forced saving and inflation taxes will limit demand by eroding real income flows and wealth. Such inflationary adjustment often occurs after adverse supply or distributional shocks. Output changes are more likely away from the bounds, especially in response to austerity programmes that reduce demand.

The WIDER studies show that both adjustment modes occur in practice. During stabilization, output contraction under austerity is the usual outcome. The IMF view is that output is determined by supply factors, so that expansionary policy risks forced saving or the inflation tax. With austerity, the Fund's central article of faith is that demand restraint does not reduce economic activity. Rather, it makes the price level (at least for non-traded goods) fall. If traded goods prices are held constant by the law of one price, then in the Fund's preferred model non-traded prices must decline with austerity. The relative price shift will improve the trade account by cutting import demand and stimulating exports. This mechanism underpins financial programming, as we will see later. Its effectiveness, unfortunately, is open to question. As already noted in Chapter 2, anyone who practices applied economics soon recognizes the irrelevance of long chains of reasoning to actual events—many linkages mean that one (or more) can readily fail. The Fund line on austerity strings together supply-determined output, constant velocity, the law of one price, and strong substitution response. If any link breaks, austerity will reduce output directly, by-passing the resource reallocation upon which the IMF relies.

4. If output adjustment is the rule, then one can ask whether progressive income redistribution will make economic activity rise or fall (or whether the economy is stagnationist or exhilarationist in the jargon introduced in Chapter 3). A similar question arises with regard to income redistribution via changing food prices that help or hurt farmers' incomes. Demand for urban/industrial products can adjust either way in response to (say) higher agricultural terms-of-trade.

The Bretton Woods view is that when the economy is not output-constrained, it is exhilarationist. Cutting real wages will generate employment and narrow the trade deficit. And although the sign of the effect on aggregate demand of changes in the terms of trade has been debated at least since the days of Malthus and Ricardo, the Fund sees the intersectoral income distribution as macroeconomically insignificant and beneath consideration. In contrast, several WIDER papers (for India, Colombia, Peru, Tanzania, and elsewhere) emphasize the macroeconomic implications of intersectoral distributional shifts. With regard to progressive redistribution more generally, most of the authors suggest that their economies adjust in stagnationist fashion.

5. In the short run, devaluation tends to be inflationary by driving up intermediate import costs and thereby final goods prices through mark-ups. The higher prices cut real wages while devaluation itself reduces national purchasing power when imports initially exceed exports. At the same time, real depreciation may stimulate import substitution and an export response. Through the first two channels devaluation will make output contract, especially in a stagnationist economy. Better trade performance may make GDP go up. Whether devaluation is contractionary or expansionary (and over what time periods) has been widely debated in developing countries in recent years. If it is contractionary, the current account improvement it induces comes from lower intermediate imports due to the output drop.

The country studies suggest that devaluation often does cause stagflation (rising prices, falling output), especially in the first year or so after it occurs. The Fund/Bank view is that devaluation is expansionary, without a doubt. It may not even cause inflation if, for example, 'rents' on import quotas make up a substantial share of income. The argument is that raising import prices will just wipe the rents out, without affecting the overall price level or aggregate demand. The structuralist *riposte* is that even with quotas, price deflation is improbable without output contraction as well.

6. Devaluation has other economy-wide repercussions, depending on institutional circumstances. In primary exporting countries it is a tool of fiscal policy—the cash flow of state marketing boards depends on the difference between producer prices and the exchange-rate determined border price of export crops. Elsewhere, wealth effects may be important. Aggregate demand probably fell no further than it did in Mexico after 1982 because devaluation increased the value of capital that had flown across the border in peso terms, stimulating spending on the part of rentiers. The country studies emphasize such linkages; the Bretton Woods approach is to talk them down in favour of price-induced substitution effects.

7. One can further ask whether devaluation and other price policies will improve tradability (reduce import coefficients and increase export market penetration) by themselves. Alternatively, is devaluation effective only in connection with other policies such as

agricultural research and technical assistance, public investment and sector-specific interventions such as directed credit, import tariff holidays for exporters, export country and commodity targeting along South Korean lines of the 1960s and 1970s, and so on?

The Bretton Woods view is that devaluation and other price signals do not require complementary interventions to work. The WIDER country authors are diametrically opposed.

8. The import content of investment in developing countries is high—at least a third almost everywhere and approaching two-thirds in sub-Saharan Africa. This technical constraint means that trade gains from reduced capital goods imports can be substantial under austerity when increased domestic activity and/or state capital formation crowd private investment in. Tight fiscal and monetary policy will force both activity and public investment to fall; devaluation may cut output as well. With crowding-in, private investment and associated imports will drop sharply during stabilization. Such a loss of animal spirits is less likely if public projects crowd private capital formation out.

The IMF approach is that any public spending crowds private investment out. Accelerator linkages will be weak assuming full employment: price and profitability signals drive the economy in near-optimal style. The WIDER studies take the opposite tack.

9. A final question with regard to the exchange rate is whether it is seriously overvalued or not. If so, the case for remedial devaluation is strong since it is very hard to run an open economy when the exchange rate is badly out of line. If the real rate is roughly 'right', then a case can be made against devaluation more rapid than the current inflation rate because of the possible stagflationary effects mentioned in point 5. Depreciating more slowly than inflation, of course, makes the dangers of overvaluation even more present. An inflation-paced path of devaluation by small steps amounts to a 'passive' crawling peg.

The IMF presumably feels that by the time it gets called in there is likely to be overvaluation. The WIDER studies suggest that the exchange rate is not always out of line at the beginning of a stabilization attempt. When present, overvaluation was the outcome of bad luck (foreign bonanzas that ended) and/or bad policies pursued by economic teams of both orthodox and populist stripe. Structuralist economists have no monopoly on not getting the exchange rate right.

10. Trade liberalization may stimulate output (at least in the medium run) by creating neoclassical economic efficiency gains. It may also hold down inflation if the law of one price broadly applies. Such views are typically Bretton Woods. By contrast, the WIDER studies suggest that liberalization may force de-industrialization if it draws in imports and not have much effect on inflation if the law of one price is not enforced by a visible presence of price-competitive traded goods in the system. Anti-liberal policies such as import quotas and export subsidies have positive effects under these circumstances. Colombia and Kenya provide successful test cases.

11. Reducing domestic absorption may or may not stimulate exports. The WIDER studies suggest that increased sales abroad are more likely if the economy has a well-established industrial base. The Fund view is that lower absorption helps trade performance everywhere.

12. Exchange liberalization may facilitate capital inflows and create financial depth. On the downside, it can permit capital flight and precipitate financial collapse. The WIDER studies present examples of the latter events, as well as situations like Colombia's and Brazil's where exchange restrictions held down capital flight. The Bank and Fund feel that because it removes distortions, exchange liberalization should be pursued.

13. Interest rate hikes typically reduce aggregate demand in the short run. Will they also be inflationary, by driving up working capital finance costs? Several WIDER studies report that stagflation after interest rate increases in their economies is observed. The IMF line is that such outcomes never occur.

14. How fragile is the domestic financial system? Has liberalization created possibilities for instability? Is a bubble likely, signalled by an excess of potential savings flows over stagnant investment demand? Or has financial stress already surfaced, requiring regulation and perhaps a bail-out of firms and banks with unhappy balance sheets? The WIDER authors recount the country histories along these lines. The IMF view is that financial fragility is not likely to be a problem if appropriately austere monetary policy is pursued. Deregulation, in particular, does not blow up bubbles.

15. The WIDER studies suggest that sometimes acceptance of an orthodox stabilization package unlocks capital inflows and sometimes not. Distinctly heterodox programmes as in Korea and

Argentina have been supported by foreign loans. What is the likely situation in the country at hand? The Fund asserts that acceptance of (and compliance with) an orthodox package is close to being a necessary and sufficient condition for drawing capital flows to a stabilizing economy. This view is at variance with the facts.

5.2 Financial Programming

Fifteen questions about how the economy functions is a good number at which to stop, although the interrogation could be extended. For present purposes the key observation is that a well-determined macro theory is implicit in the way that the Fund and Bank resolve our contrasts—they have a coherent view about how developing economies work. An explicit representation in model form will be presented shortly. But before we go into that it bears repeating that Bretton Woods orthodoxy is a special case. A response to any of the 15 questions along the lines suggested by the WIDER authors opens doors to policies that do not often appear in Letters of Intent. The operational challenge is to find ways in which alternative approaches to stabilization can be implemented in practical terms.

New ideas enter establishment thinking at best gradually. Especially in an institution as hermetic as the International Monetary Fund, percolation of alternative ways of viewing the world is bound to be slow. After all, Fund packages have been based on just one formal model now for 30 years, after an initial statement by Jacques Polak (1957). Certainly in terms of the numbers of countries and people it has affected, Polak's work is the most important piece of macroeconomics since Keynes. As such it merits substantial respect. In what follows we first set out the specification of the model as it is usually applied, before suggesting changes that might make the Fund approach fit macroeconomic reality better in the Third World.[2]

The genius of the Polak Model (or financial programming in the

[2] There are several recent papers restating the financial programming methodology and suggesting improvements. The analysis in this chapter follows Taylor (1987c) and especially Bacha (1987). The Bretton Woods agencies have also taken up the challenge of revising their methods, as in the proposals by Khan, Montiel, and Haque (1986) from the Bank and Chad (1987) from the Fund. Unfortunately, these authors retain the neoclassical/monetarist 'full employment' assumption that output is determined solely from the side of the supply. That makes their discussions of austerity, devaluation, structural inflation, and other problems a bit beside the point.

jargon of the Fund) is that it is built around the accounting identities for the banking system, balance of payments, and government budget that every country uses as part of its macroeconomic data base. There are four main elements—the three identities just mentioned plus a definitional tautology. The first identity is the consolidated balance sheet of the banking system. It equates liabilities to assets, or

(1)   money supply = international reserves + domestic bank credit

Second, we have the tautology—our old friend the equation of exchange (or quantity theory of money), stating that

(2)   money demand = price level × output/velocity

in which 'velocity' is defined as a scale factor between the stock of money and the current flow value of production.

As we have seen repeatedly, typical monetarist hypotheses are that output is set from the supply side and velocity is an institutionally determined constant in the short run. The simplest version of open economy monetarism further presumes that the law of one price applies, so that the overall price level is predetermined. If the money market continuously clears then the sum of reserves and domestic credit must equal the value of output divided by velocity. The reserve level becomes the only possible dependent variable in the demand–supply equation. The first theorem of the IMF, so to speak, is that if credit creation exceeds a value consistent with money demand treated as a function of national income, then international reserves will fall. A good external performance depends on domestic credit restraint.

We can restate this result in terms of the balance of payments, the third main ingredient in financial programming. By definition, the current account is the surplus of nominal income (price level × output) over the value of domestic spending or absorption,

(3)   current account = price × output − absorption

From the overall balance of payments we can also write

(4)   current account = change in reserves − capital inflows

Putting these equations together with (1) and (2) expressed in terms of changes in their variables over time leads to

(5)   absorption − price × output = increase in domestic
         credit − increase in money demand + capital inflows

where the change in money demand follows from projections of the variables on the right-hand side of (2) and capital inflows are assumed to be predetermined.

This second theorem of accounting seems to show that if absorption exceeds income on the left-hand side of the 'equals' sign, then there must be more credit creation (net of capital inflows) than new money demand. From (3) there will be a deficit on the current account. With the restrictions we have imposed (constant output and velocity, price level fixed from abroad), the implication for policy is that limiting credit creation is the only way to force absorption to conform to income, thus assuring a healthy current account. Equation (5) is the basis for computing the limits on domestic credit that figure in all Letters of Intent that borrowing countries sign with the Fund.

The credit targets are typically further detailed in terms of the statement of uses and sources of funds of the government, the final account used in financial programming. It states that

(6)   government spending − government revenue = capital
         inflows + increase in domestic bank credit to the government

on the assumptions that the state does the bulk of the economy's borrowing abroad and that it cannot place its domestic liabilities outside the banking system.

With capital inflows predetermined and total domestic credit creation following from (5), limiting the fiscal deficit on the left-hand side of (6) will hold down state credit demand and so avoid crowding the private sector out of financial markets. If private credit demand is cut too drastically, the Fund argument runs, then output may suffer. Empirically this point is well-founded—just recall the case of the Philippines discussed in Chapter 4. The Fund views itself as guarding against private credit squeezes by using (6) to set performance criteria for the public sector borrowing requirement (or PSBR) in most Letters of Intent. Sometimes suggestions about specific fiscal moves are added to assure that the PSBR target will be reached. Problems of overkill arise because Fund staff members ignore the redistributive or contractionary effects of the other tools in their collection. They view the world in self-consistent terms; the problem is that their assumptions about the means by which the accounting identities for money, the balance of payments, and the government budget are satisfied differ from the adjustment mechanisms one observes repeatedly in the Third World.

Besides setting fiscal and credit limits, we have seen that IMF programmes typically aim at reducing inflation, and also incorporate devaluation, liberalization, and incomes policies. These extensions stretch the limits of financial programming strictly defined. It pays to write down a few more equations to see how Fund country economists fit these extra features into their programmes, before suggesting how improvements can be made.

The preferred IMF inflation theory would obviously be a restatement of (1) and (2) as

(7)   price level = money supply × velocity/output

or the same equation set out in growth rate form with constant velocity

(8)   inflation rate = growth rate of money supply − growth rate of
                        output

A seeming contradiction arises in that (7) and (8) are inconsistent with the law of one price: the price level cannot be determined by both the money supply and foreign trade relations at the same time. In formal models, this problem evaporates if we distinguish traded and non-traded goods, as signalled in the last section and elaborated shortly. In practice, IMF economists sidestep it by setting credit limits with one eye on the balance of payments and the other on inflation.

An IMF forecast of the inflation rate in most programme economies is well below the current rate, and proves to be an underestimate of the rate observed after the projection.[3] If this target were to be satisfied then the financial programming exercise would go through as previously discussed. If observed inflation

---

[3] This bias shows up repeatedly in the WIDER studies and is verified econometrically by Kenan (1986), who shows that the Fund staff consistently underestimate the inflation rate and overestimate the growth rate in developing countries.

exceeds the target—the common case—then the real demand injection from nominally fixed state spending will decline, while forced saving and/or inflation taxes will hold consumer spending down. However, output is still being held constant in the Fund's thought experiments, so that the demand reduction will slow price increases. By substitution responses to be discussed shortly, the current account should improve. So whether that target is met or not, their model's outcomes ratify the Fund staff's fixation on credit limits as a cure for both inflation and balance of payments disease.

Cutting the current account deficit by restraining the price level ties in with devaluation, if one reasons in terms of a sectoral disaggregation between traded and non-traded goods. This distinction is hard to draw empirically. However, as we saw in our third contrast above, its logic is simple. Suppose that the overall price level is held down by credit restraint in (7). If the law of one price applies then non-traded prices must decline. The real exchange rate, defined as the ratio of traded to non-traded prices, will depreciate, leading to reduced imports and stronger exports. Nominal devaluation will accentuate the process by boosting traded goods prices. Substitution should be faster and go further, since an overall limit to price movements is set by the equation of exchange. As usual, these Fund deductions omit the possibility that output instead of prices may respond to austerity or exchange rate changes. They invoke the suspiciously long chains of economic reasoning that we discussed in connection with contrast number three above.

Incomes policies enter the package if we bring in the simplest decomposition of the value of output into its cost components:

(9)   price × output = profits + wage bill + intermediate import
             costs + cost of financing working capital

If profits are to be maintained to assure medium-run growth while import costs are increased by devaluation, (9) shows that the wage bill will have to be held down to permit an inflation target to be met. Fund economists lobby for incomplete wage indexation to past inflation on these grounds. Their computations are rarely set out for public discussion, but typically rely on the underestimates of price increases already discussed. The Mexican case in Chapter 4 shows that the forecast arithmetic is not always done right.

Finally, interest rate increases and liberalization of trade and exchange restrictions are put into Fund/Bank packages more as a statement of faith in market mechanisms than a well-articulated programme, although calculations of effective rates of protection and domestic resource costs provide some guidance about which distortions are the 'worst'. The relevance of these exercises is questioned in Section 5.4.

5.3 Improving the Methodology

As with the Bretton Woods interpretation of the 15 points discussed previously, financial programming is an internally consistent way of looking at the economy. Its major problems are that it ignores (or assumes away) output variation and determination of prices from the side of costs. The financial approach directs attention to the banking system, external balance, and government finance. It ignores autonomous elements on the right-hand side of the cost decomposition (9) and the fact that both output and absorption will depend on themselves and other variables in the system via income–expenditure linkages.

The only way to make financial programming complete is to add the missing macroeconomic equations, preferably in the simplest form possible. For price determination, we can use a mark-up rule:

(10)   price level = mark-up rate × prime cost

where

(11)   prime cost = wage rate × (labour/output) + (exchange rate × intermediate imports/output) + cost of financing working capital

in which the input–output ratios for labour and intermediate imports may be assumed constant and the cost of working capital finance depends on the interest rate. A growth rate version of these equations along the lines of (8) in which the price inflation rate decomposes into a weighted average of growth rates of costs is left for the avid reader to derive. A modest exercise in differentiation is required.

Equations (10) and (11) provide a cost-based theory of price determination alternative to (7). It works reasonably well for non-staple goods producing sectors when the economy is not output-constrained.[4] If some sectors are subject to production limits due to a completed harvest, capacity ceilings, or scarce foreign exchange, mark-up price equations can be complemented with a flexible-price, demand-supply analysis of these markets. With indexation of the wage and exchange rate to current or recently past rates of price increase as a propagation mechanism, a model appropriately combining mark-up and market-clearing prices embodies structuralist inflation theory. The country studies suggest that structural models fit the inflationary process at least as well as their monetarist competitors in practice.

A *first recommendation* for improving financial programming is that both theories (or a blend) should be worked into IMF country assessments. In particular, is inflation likely to be reduced by austerity, and with what effects on output by sector and over what time horizon? Another way to phrase the question is in terms of output elasticities. How far will economic activity have to drop to force the mark-up rate or some other component of cost to decline enough to slow inflation? Econometricians usually conclude that the elasticities of most components of cost with respect to output are very low indeed.

Income generation in a model in which output is not pre-determined follows from a restated version of (3):

(12)   price × output = absorption + exports − competitive imports

The WIDER country studies suggest that absorption here is likely to depend on several factors, which can be read from our 15 points. They include the level and distribution of income (linked in turn to input costs and output), the fiscal demand injection, and total investment which will be influenced by public capital formation and accelerator effects. Exports will depend on price variables (the exchange rate and subsidies), perhaps absorption, public interventions such as investment in export capacity, and world market conditions. Competitive imports will depend on how effectively demand in sectors open to the world is regulated. As we

---

[4] As economic activity rises (in a range below the onset of forced saving), the mark-up may vary—rising from demand pressure or perhaps even falling as fixed costs are spread over a greater value of sales. At least in the WIDER studies these changes are largely treated as second order, though they do show up in econometrics around the world.

have seen, food market conditions are often a key factor in stabilization efforts. If foreign exchange, time, and port capacity are available, excess demand conditions can be alleviated by competitive imports.

In connection with (10) and (11), equation (12) is the framework for a simple general equilibrium model which can be solved for price and quantity variables on the real side of the economy. There is no reason to build a numerical version in any country, although such exercises are illuminating when model jockeys make serious efforts to think through local relationships likely to be macroeconomically important. Putting the accounts that underlie all the identities discussed here into consistent shape is also an extremely useful endeavour. Recall the difficulties in Brazil of judging the demand injection implicit in the Cruzado Plan heterodox shock—better numbers would certainly have helped.

A *second recommendation* is that the IMF should do more macroeconomic thinking. Fund programmes should be internally consistent in the sense of satisfying the accounting in (10) to (12) with enough detail added to take into account income–expenditure feedbacks and the other linkages just discussed. As spelled out in detail in Table 1, a useful specification will have to incorporate the nature of the shocks to be stabilized, the macroeconomic adjustment modes of the economy at hand, and its specifically relevant institutional details and macroeconomic linkages. Such analysis is not difficult, and takes one much further along the road towards sensible policy than perpetual assumptions that the price level comes from an ill-defined combination of the law of one price and the equation of exchange, while output is fixed by supply.

A *third recommendation* is that the contractionary effects of Fund packages be adequately taken into account, which is likely to lead to a more diversified selection of policies. That is, if fiscal austerity, public investment cuts, devaluation, interest rate increases, and trade liberalization all can cause output loss or faster inflation through linkages observed in practice, there is no reason to impose them all at once. If foreign restrictions are truly binding, presumably one wants to add a margin of safety regarding conditions in the rest of the world—which means there is good reason to err in the direction of 'overkill'. But only employing contractionary policies scarcely makes economic sense, if as a consequence poverty and unemployment spread, productive firms go bankrupt, and the financial system becomes fragile. Recovering from such problems is immensely difficult, as demonstrated by experience in Mexico, the Southern Cone, and other countries in which orthodox remedies have been applied to the extreme. This risk can be reduced by a sensible policy mix in the short run.

Fourth, the distributional and employment implications of stabilization should be taken into account, ideally along the lines of the social matrixes of the WIDER studies, which identify relevant economic groups, their insertion into the macro system, and their political and economic interconnections. Without serious analysis along these lines, trying to bring distribution into the picture will remain a pious hope.[5]

Fifth, due attention should be paid to limitations on policy imposed by output constraints (whether from capacity, limited food supply, or foreign exchange), and badly misaligned prices. Forced saving adjustment and an overvalued exchange rate are hard to handle, and one does well to avoid them.

Sixth, thought should be devoted to real/financial linkages and their effects on stabilization. Does 'the' interest rate, for example, clear the financial market? If so what are its feedbacks to the rest of the system? If not what quantity variables adjust? How do capital movements affect domestic credit conditions—for example, will capital flight lead to substantial reserve losses and a credit squeeze? Is there a potential excess of investable funds which might blow up a speculative bubble? The country studies emphasize the importance of such possibilities. They cannot be incorporated into simple formal models and consistency exercises—all the more reason why they should not be permitted to drop from sight.

Seventh, how will stabilization fare with respect to the policy goals mentioned in Chapter 2—output, inflation, distribution, and self-reliance? Consistency computations transcending financial programming are required to give a coherent answer. They should be pursued.

---

[5] A so-called 'social accounting matrix' (or SAM) which amplifies the usual input–output table to take into account income–expenditure links can be a tool for distributional analysis, so long as disaggregation by sector, income group, etc., is not taken too far—an illuminating table easily explodes into a high-class wall-papering job. See Taylor (1983) for SAM references and an application to India.

There are two last programming issues that have to do with the medium run. One is how to find the level of external resources adequate to support growth, presumably the central task of the Bank and Fund. The second, more serious consideration is the choice of a development strategy. We take up the first immediately, and postpone the other to the following sections.

On the issue of foreign exchange limits, it is natural to rely on the well-known two-gap model.[6] Ignoring reserve changes, we can state conditions for saving–investment balance and the make-up of the current account respectively as

(13)   capital inflows = (capital/output) × output increase − (saving/output) × output

and

(14)   capital inflows = (intermediate imports/output) × output + (machine imports/investment) × (capital/output) × output increase − (exports/output) × output

The ratio terms in parentheses can be treated as parameters influenced by policy and redistributional processes such as forced saving. Three key variables then appear in (13) and (14)—the level of capital inflows and the level and increase (or growth rate) of output. The equations can be used for 'growth programming' complementary to the Fund's financial exercises. In particular, they permit one to ask in pointed fashion whether capital inflows projected for a country will enable it to reach acceptable levels of economic activity and growth.

An *eighth recommendation* is that the Fund in collaboration with country authorities (and the Bank) undertake growth programming exercises to check the medium-term implications of stabilization programmes. The task is not trivial, since a much more thorough macro analysis than that which goes into financial programming (and the Bank's current use of its RIMSIM model) is presupposed: in particular, lines of causality and specific macro linkages have to

[6] The model is basically due to Hollis Chenery—see Chenery and Strout (1966). The presentation here follows Bacha (1984) and Taylor (1983). The World Bank's Revised Standard Model (ro RIMSIM) in principle follows the two-gap specification, although in practice one or the other of equations (13) and (14) is usually suppressed, along with the structural rigidities the model was designed to point out.

be addressed instead of ignored as in present Bretton Woods practice. But the agencies' seal of approval for capital inflows is really not of much use unless one has more than a mechanical (and often biased) projection of how large the forex contribution has to be.

5.4 Other Perspectives

As we noted in Chapter 1, the past ten years or so have been exceptionally turbulent for the Third World. Since they are charged by the international system to deal with that turbulence, the Fund and Bank have become correspondingly visible on the world stage. It is not surprising that their roles have been closely scrutinized. This section is devoted to some of the outcomes of that scrutiny. The first topic considered is the effect of stabilization on human welfare. Then we take up distinctions between the rhetoric and the actions of the two institutions, and close with contrasts between their apparent world-views and those of others.

With regard to its effects on the ways that people live, the IMF package of policies in particular has been widely criticized. Unemployment and regressive changes in the income distribution have clearly been associated with Fund programmes, in the countries included in the WIDER project and elsewhere. For example, evidence is provided by a recent UNICEF project on 'adjustment with a human face', as discussed by Cornia, Jolly, and Stewart (1987) and Pinstrup-Andersen (1987). Both sources, while stressing the difficulty of firmly establishing causal links, document reductions in government outreach and social service activities, increases or reduced rates of decrease in observed indexes of malnutrition and public ill health (such as the infant mortality rate), and general deterioration in living standards.

In their own defence the Bretton Woods agencies quite correctly observe that given the magnitude of macroeconomic shocks suffered by poor countries their citizens were bound to suffer. For example, an article by Tseng (1984) in *Finance and Development*, the Fund's and Bank's popular publication, points out that '. . . the costs of adjustment, therefore, must be seen in perspective. In the short run, the costs are the unavoidable sacrifices that accompany the correction of an unsustainable situation.' In an earlier presentation of IMF methodology, Khan and Knight (1981) concede that '. . . programs designed to achieve quick results on the balance of payments via sharp deflation are likely to have significant and undesirable effects on output, employment, and factor incomes, particularly in the short run.' The striking thing about these quotations is not so much that they recognize reality for what it is, but that they imply that IMF-type policies will make an unpleasant short-run position better quite soon. The WIDER and UNICEF studies demonstrate that the economic situation (especially that of the poor) in developing countries often continues to deteriorate under Bretton Woods ministrations. Judging from their past performance, one wonders whether the agencies do not know what they are doing, or prefer not to inform a gravely ill collection of patients just how bad their conditions may be.[7]

The UNICEF authors suggest an alternative policy package to deal with distribution problems: a more expansionary macro stance, pursuit of 'meso' policies to support disadvantaged groups and restructure the economy, adoption of new technologies in the social sector (such as oral rehydration therapy for cholera and low-cost health delivery systems more generally), direct compensatory programmes such as public works schemes to benefit groups that have been badly affected, and improved welfare monitoring. Such interventions are certainly in line with those proposed by the authors in the WIDER project, and the two approaches should be seen as complementary. What differences exist, perhaps, lie in different views about the propagation of inequality. Poverty and an unequal welfare distribution in some countries are built into their social matrixes and macroeconomic systems. The unlamented Somoza period in Nicaragua provides a graphic example; readers can no doubt add their own in the world of today. The essentially palliative UNICEF package will have at best partial success until the root causes of poverty are attacked. Needless to say, the Bretton Woods agencies are not (and should not be) in the revolutionary line of endeavour. But they certainly could give palliation a try.

Between the agencies themselves there are also contrasts which

---

[7] One hears Fund and Bank staff members at conferences and informal gatherings adopting the 'wise old doctor' approach, saying that they have at times lied to their 'patients' for their own good. Apparently they do not realize that this ancient custom vanished from Western medicine with the generation of doctors that entered practice not long after World War II.

evolve over time. The broadbrush picture is that the Fund *stabilizes* on the basis of a monetarist model like that set out in equations (1) to (9) while the Bank tries to help countries *adjust* in the medium term along semi-articulated lines which stress the need to enhance supply by investment—the two-gap approach of equations (13) and (14)—plus price policy. Since the mid-1970s these models have overlapped more than they did in the past, as attempted stabilizations stretch on and on. In recent Bretton Woods theory (e.g. the papers cited in footnote 2), Fund and Bank models are seen as complementary. In practice they often are not, with tension between the respective staffs occasionally verging on open warfare (as in several countries in the WIDER sample).

Each agency has itself evolved, the Bank more than the Fund. The IMF has always been more self-contained; at least its official pronouncements change little over time. A recent example presented at a conference devoted to assessing Bank and Fund programmes—Guitian (1987)—aside from contemporary citations might as well have been written twenty years ago. But at the same time Fund leadership was essential in rounding up finance for the Third World after the debt shock and staff publications like the annual *World Economic Outlook* are quite clear on how objectively difficult the poor countries' situation is. At the level of forming country policy, as we will see, there are hints of change, but they are slow in coming.

The Bank's rhetoric and practice have gone in opposite directions in the past ten years. Conservative governments in the main stockholders—the industrial countries—have seen their views reflected in the Bank's spotlighted publications. Recent numbers of the annual *World Development Report*, for example, verge on exaltation in their advocacy of market-oriented, hands-off policies. At the same time, at least in some activities such as Structural Adjustment Loans to Turkey and sub-Saharan Africa, the Bank has pursued a line of intelligent conservatism. Recent African packages rely on ample balance of payments support to permit an immediate import increase, positive GDP growth, some public investment, and even the maintenance of public and private consumption. Also, in the field, Bank sectoral staff have always been more sensible than their latest in-house theoreticians. These tendencies go in the directions advocated by the WIDER country authors; in the

African context they have also been associated with a less austere approach by the Fund. The implications there are that extreme short-run contraction is best avoided, but at the same time long-term external resource inflows (at least in absolute amounts if not as percentages of GDP) may be required.

These developments suggest that economic and contextual realities do penetrate minds in the Bank and (to a lesser extent) the Fund. The obvious question, then, is how deep does the penetration go? There is no doubt that the staff members of the agencies now display a strong market-oriented bias in what they say. This has always been true in the IMF, and certainly in the post-McNamara years in the Bank. As far as actions go, the WIDER studies amply document the historically doctrinaire nature (with occasional exceptions) of IMF policy practice. The Bank, again, has always been more ambivalent and labile.

Contemporary market-oriented Bretton Woods propaganda reflects recent trends in economics as a whole. Indeed, development is probably the profession's only sub-field in which alternative perspectives contend. As a recent survey article puts the issue:

Development economics as a separate branch of economics originated in a widespread perception of the limited usefulness of orthodox economics, and even though its pristine separateness has mellowed over the years it retains to this day its contrary, unruly, if somewhat flaky, image in the eyes of mainstream economists. Standard neoclassical economics is mainly on the defensive in this terrain . . .[8]

While the last assertion is perhaps too optimistic with regard to alternative perspectives, the quotation rings true.

The history is briefly that a neoclassical reaction to previous views took shape around 1970, and has steadily become more important over time. From a structuralist perspective, the discussion herein amounts to an attempted rebuttal on the field of stabilization policy. With regard to medium-term growth, as we have noted in passing, the mainstream largely emphasizes that liberalization and export promotion are the strategies to be pursued. Empirically, these assertions rest on shaky ground. There is no very clear association between either Manchester liberalism or an export push and growth (Taylor 1987a). Specific country cases can always

[8] Bardhan 1988.

be found, but on both sides of the issue. The agencies do not know what they are doing when they advocate liberalism as a necessary or even sufficient condition for long-term economic progress.

5.5 Questions of Strategy

These observations set the stage for final considerations about development strategy. Specifically, will an orthodox stabilization package coupled with liberalization plus a modicum of directed investment and public intervention lead an economy towards stable, egalitarian long-run growth? Obviously no full answer to such a question can be given, but a few comments can be made.

First, the risk of economic collapse under liberalization seems to be non-trivial, if recent history in the Southern Cone, Mexico, and African countries such as Zaire provides a guide.

Second, an austere policy contains no natural transition to development in the long term once one departs from simplistic, savings-driven neoclassical growth models. Historically, sources of growth have taken the form of capital formation and technical advance. Neither investment nor innovation is stimulated by stagnation. That is why the recent expansive African stabilizations carry more seeds for success than did the simple IMF recessions of the past.

Third, the partially successful country outcomes in the WIDER sample—Turkey, Sri Lanka, Kenya, Colombia, Argentina, Peru, South Korea, Ghana—were all based upon stabilization packages combining price signals and directed state intervention, with getting prices right playing a secondary role. The non-central role of removing distortions is also apparent in long-term expansion in South Korea, Brazil, and elsewhere (Pack and Westphal 1986). What happened in one country—with its accumulated history of economic change, distributional conflict, policy, and politics—provides no sure guide about what to do somewhere else or in the same place later in time. But even if the details are not transferable, the orientation of successful stabilization seems clear. It goes towards hands-on public management of a mixed economic system, and not wholesale liberalization moves.

Fourth, public intervention (the 'human face') is required to sustain welfare. At the same time, distributional conflicts and the current political situation tightly constrain policy. To find the degrees of freedom that exist, institutional awareness is essential. It is not always displayed by economists, from the Bank and Fund or elsewhere.

Fifth, policy depends on context. The best Bretton Woods economists have always practised this precept; their inferior colleagues have been too willing to fall back on financial programming and the certainties of the latest World Bank line. These defences will erode as developing country economists—the authors of the WIDER studies among others—surpass the visitors from the North in knowledge and technique. This passing of the ships has already occurred in many countries, and in part is responsible for recent changes in the Bank and Fund. These tendencies will only grow stronger with time.

Finally, at its best the Bretton Woods approach is based on overly rigid theory about macroeconomics in the Third World, alleviated by common sense. The WIDER papers show that more realistic theoretical formulations are at hand. In time they will even be in common parlance along 19th Street in Washington DC, where (for good institutional reasons) novel ideas always take a long time to arrive.

REFERENCES

Abdel-Khalek, Gouda (1987) 'Recent Stabilization Experience in Egypt: Redistribution without Growth?' Helsinki: WIDER

Amadeo, Edward (1986) *Keynes's Principle of Effective Demand and Its Relationship to Alternative Theories of Distribution and Accumulation*, Cambridge, Ma: Department of Economics, Harvard University (unpublished PhD dissertation)

Amsden, Alice H. (1987) 'Growth and Stabilization in Korea, 1962–84', Helsinki: WIDER

Arellano, Jose Pablo, Rene Cortazar, and Andres Solimano (1986) 'Adjustment Policies in Chile: 1981–85', Helsinki: WIDER

Arida, Persio (1986) 'Macroeconomic Issues for Latin America', *Journal of Development Economics*, 22: 171–208

Arida, Persio, and Andre Lara-Resende (1985) 'Inertial Inflation and Monetary Reform in Brazil', in John Williamson (ed.) *Indexation and Inflation: Argentina, Brazil, and Israel*, Washington, DC: Institute for International Economics

Avramovic, Dragoslav (1986) 'Conditionality: Facts, Theory, and Policy', Washington, DC: Bank of Credit and Commerce International

Bacha, Edmar L. (1984) 'Growth with Limited Supplies of Foreign Exchange: A Reappraisal of the Two-Gap Model', in Moshe Syrquin, Lance Taylor, and Larry Westphal (eds.) *Economic Structure and Performance: Essays in Honor of Hollis B. Chenery*, New York: Academic Press

——(1987) 'The Design of IMF Conditionality: A Reform Proposal', Rio de Janeiro: Departamento de Economia, Pontificia Universidade Catolica

Barbone, Luca (1985) *Essays on Trade and Macro Policy in Developing Countries*, Cambridge, Ma: Department of Economics, Massachusetts Institute of Technology (unpublished PhD dissertation)

Bardhan, Pranab (1988) 'Alternative Approaches to Development Economics', in Hollis B. Chenery and T. N. Srinivasan (eds.) *Handbook of Development Economics*, vol. I, Amsterdam: North-Holland

Boratav, Korkut (1986) 'Distribution, External Linkages and Growth under Orthodox Policies: The Turkish Economy in the Early 1980s', Helsinki: WIDER

Canvese, Alfredo (1982) 'The Structuralist Explanation in the Theory of Inflation', *World Development*, 10: 523–9

Carneiro, Dionisio Dias (1987) 'Stabilization Policies and Long-Run Adjustment: The Brazilian Economy in the Eighties', Helsinki: WIDER

Cavallo, Domingo (1977) *Stagflationary Effects of Monetarist Stabilization Policies*, Cambridge, Ma: Department of Economics, Harvard University (unpublished PhD dissertation)

Chand, Sheetal K. (1987) 'Toward a Growth-Oriented Model of Financial Programming', Washington, DC: International Monetary Fund

Chenery, Hollis B., and Alan M. Strout (1966) 'Foreign Assistance and Economic Development', *American Economic Review*, 56: 679–733

Choucri, Nazli (1985) 'A Study of Sudanese Nationals Working Abroad: Final Report', Cambridge, Ma: Department of Political Science, Massachusetts Institute of Technology

——and Supriya Lahiri (1984) 'Short Run Energy-Economy Interactions in Egypt', *World Development*, 12: 789–820

Cooper, Richard N. (1971) 'Currency Devaluation in Developing Countries', Princeton, NJ: *Essays in International Finance*, no. 86

Corden, W. M. (1984) 'Booming Sector and Dutch Disease Economics: Survey and Consolidation', *Oxford Economic Papers*, 36: 359–80

Cornia, Giovanni, Richard Jolly, and Frances Stewart (1987) *Adjustment with a Human Face*, Oxford: Clarendon Press

Diaz-Alejandro, Carlos F. (1963) 'A Note on the Impact of Devaluation and the Redistributive Effect', *Journal of Political Economy*, 71: 577–80

——(1981) 'Southern Cone Stabilization Plans', in William Cline and Sidney Weintraub (eds.) *Economic Stabilization in Developing Countries*, Washington, DC: Brookings Institute

Dutt, Amitava K. (1984) 'Stagnation, Income Distribution, and Monopoly Power', *Cambridge Journal of Economics*, 8: 25–40

Fisher, Irving (1933) 'The Debt-Deflation Theory of Great Depressions', *Econometrica*, 1: 337–57

Franco, Gustavo (1986) *Aspects of the Economics of Hyperinflations: Theoretical Issues and Historical Studies of Four European Hyperinflations in the 1920s*, Cambridge, Ma: Department of Economics, Harvard University (unpublished PhD dissertation)

Frenkel, Roberto (1983) 'Mercado Financiero, Expectativas Cambiales, y Movimientos de Capital', *Trimestre Economico*, 50: 2041–76

——, Jose Maria Fanelli, and Carlos Winograd (1987) 'Stabilization and Adjustment Programs and Policies in Argentina', Helsinki: WIDER

Galbraith, John Kenneth (1957) 'Market Structure and Stabilization Policy', *Review of Economics and Statistics*, 31: 50–3

Gibson, Bill (1986) '(de) Stabilization Policy in Nicaragua', Helsinki: WIDER

——, Nora Lustig, and Lance Taylor (1986) 'Terms of Trade and Class Conflict in a Computable General Equilibrium Model for Mexico', *Journal of Development Studies*, **23**: 40–59

Giovannini, Alberto (1985) 'Saving and the Real Interest Rate in LDCs', *Journal of Development Economics*, **18**: 197–217

Green, Reginald Herbold (1987) 'Ghana: Stabilization and Structural Shifts', Helsinki: WIDER

——and Xavier Kadhani (1986) 'Zimbabwe: Transition to Economic Crisis, 1981–83: Retrospect and Prospect', *World Development*, **14**: 1059–83

Guitian, Manuel (1987) 'Adjustment and Economic Growth: Their Fundamental Complementarity', Washington, DC: International Monetary Fund

Harris, John R. (1986) 'Macroeconomic Adjustment in Sudan, 1972–85', Helsinki: WIDER

Helleiner, G. K. (1987) 'Foreign Direct Investment and Balance of Payments Adjustment in Latin America', Toronto: Department of Economics, University of Toronto

Hicks, John R. (1965) *Capital and Growth*, Oxford: Clarendon Press

Hirschman, Albert O. (1949) 'Devaluation and the Trade Balance: A Note', *Review of Economics and Statistics*, **31**: 50–3

Jayawardena, Lal, Anne Maasland, and P. N. Radhakrishnan (1988) 'Case Study on Sri Lanka', Helsinki: WIDER

Kaldor, Nicholas (1955) 'Alternative Theories of Distribution', *Review of Economic Studies*, **23**: 83–100

——(1976) 'Inflation and Recession in the World Economy', *Economic Journal*, **86**: 703–14

Kalecki, Michal (1965) *Theory of Economic Dynamics* (2nd edition), London: Allen and Unwin

——(1971) *Selected Essays on the Dynamics of the Capitalist Economy*, Cambridge: Cambridge University Press

Kamin, Stephen (1987) *Devaluation, External Balance and Macroeconomic Performance in Developing Countries*, Cambridge, Ma: Department of Economics, Massachusetts Institute of Technology (unpublished PhD dissertation)

Kenan, Peter (1986) 'International Money and Macroeconomics; An Agenda for Research', Princeton, NJ: Department of Economics, Princeton University

Khan, Mohsin, and Malcolm D. Knight (1981) 'Stabilization in Developing Countries: A Formal Framework', *International Monetary Fund Staff Papers*, **28**: 1–53

——, Peter Montiel, and Nadeem U. Haque (1986) 'Adjustment with

Growth: Relating the Analytical Approaches of the World Bank and the IMF', Washington, DC: World Bank

Krugman, Paul, and Lance Taylor (1978) 'Contractionary Effects of Devaluation', *Journal of International Economics*, 8: 445–56

Kindleberger, Charles P. (1978) *Manias, Panics, and Crashes: A History of Financial Crises*, New York: Basic Books

——(1985) *Keynesianism vs. Monetarism and Other Essays in Financial History*, London: Allen and Unwin

Lal, Deepak (1987) 'The Political Economy of Economic Liberalization', *World Bank Economic Review*, 1: 273–99

Lopes, Francisco (1984) 'Inflacao Inercial, Hiperinflacao, e Disinflacao: Notas e Conjecturas', Rio de Janeiro: Departamento de Economia, Pontificia Universidade Catolica

Lopez Portillo, Jose (1982) *Informe Presidencial*, Mexico City: Government of Mexico

Lora, Eduardo, and Jose Antonio Ocampo (1986) 'Economic Activity, Macroeconomic Policy, and Income Distribution in Colombia, 1980–1990', Helsinki: WIDER

Lustig, Nora, and Jaime Ros (1987) 'Stabilization and Adjustment in Mexico, 1982–1985', Helsinki: WIDER

Maasland, Anne (1987) 'Continuing the Tradition of Equity in Sri Lanka: An Application of a Computable General Equilibrium Model', Cambridge, Ma: Department of Economics, Massachusetts Institute of Technology

McKinnon, Ronald I. (1973) *Money and Capital in Economic Development*, Washington, DC: Brookings Institution

Marglin, Stephen (1985) *Growth, Distribution, and Prices*, Cambridge, Ma: Harvard University Press

Modiano, Eduardo (1987) 'El Plan Cruzado: Bases Teoricas y Limitaciones Practicas', *Trimestre Economico*, 54: special issue

Montes, Manuel F. (1987) 'Macroeconomic Adjustment in the Philippines, 1983–85', Helsinki: WIDER

Morales, Juan Antonio (1987) 'Estabilizacion y Nueva Politica Economica en Bolivia', *Trimestre Economico*, 54: special issue

Morley, Samuel (1971) 'Inflation and Stagflation in Brazil', *Economic Development and Cultural Change*, 19: 184–203

Ndulu, Benno (1987) 'Stabilization and Adjustment Programs in Tanzania, 1978–1985', Helsinki: WIDER

Noyola Vasquez, Juan F. (1956) 'El Desarrollo Economico y la Inflacion en Mexico y Otros Paises Latinoamericanos', *Investigacion Economica*, 16: 603–48

Ocampo, Jose Antonio (1987a) 'The Macroeconomic Effect of Import

Controls: A Keynesian Analysis', *Journal of Development Economics*, **27**: 285–306

——(1987b) 'Una Evaluacion Comparativa de Cuatro Planes Anti-Inflacionarios Recientes', *Trimestre Economico*, **54**: special issue

Okun, Arthur (1981) *Prices and Quantities: A Macroeconomic Analysis*, Washington, DC: Brookings Institution

Olivera, Julio (1967) 'Money, Prices, and Fiscal Lags: A Note on the Dynamics of Inflation', *Banco Nazionale del Lavoro Quarterly Review*, **20**: 258–67

Pack, Howard, and Larry E. Westphal (1986) 'Industrial Strategy and Technological Change: Theory vs. Reality', *Journal of Development Economics*, **22**: 87–128

Pegatienan Hiey, Jacques (1987) 'Recent and Future Stabilization Experience in the Ivory Coast', Helsinki: WIDER

Pinstrup-Andersen, Per (1987) 'Macroeconomic Adjustment Policies and Human Nutrition: Available Evidence and Research Needs', Washington, DC: International Food Policy Research Institute

Polak, J. J. (1957) 'Monetary Analysis of Income Formation and Payments Problems', *International Monetary Fund Staff Papers*, **6**: 1–50

Ros, Jaime (1987) 'On the Macroeconomics of Heterodox Shocks', Helsinki: WIDER

Rowthorn, Bob (1982) 'Demand, Real Wages, and Economic Growth', *Studi Economici*, no. 18, 2–53

Sachs, Jeffrey D. (1987) 'Trade and Exchange Rate Policies in Growth-Oriented Adjustment Programs', Cambridge, Ma: Department of Economics, Harvard University

Sarkar, Hiren, and Manoj Panda (1986) 'Administered Prices, Inflation, and Growth: Some Results for Indian Economy', New Delhi: National Council for Applied Economic Research

Sen, Abhijit (1981) *The Agrarian Constraint to Economic Development: The Case of India*, Cambridge: Faculty of Economics and Politics, University of Cambridge (unpublished PhD dissertation)

Sen, Amartya K. (1963) 'Neo-Classical and Neo-Keynesian Theories of Distribution', *Economic Record*, **39**: 54–64

Sen, Pronab (1987) 'Indian Experiences with Orthodox Stabilization', Helsinki: WIDER

Shaw, Edward S. (1973) *Financial Deepening in Economic Development*, New York: Oxford University Press

Sraffa, Piero (1960) *Production of Commodities by Means of Commodities*, Cambridge: Cambridge University Press

Steindl, Josef (1952) *Maturity and Stagnation in American Capitalism*, Oxford: Basil Blackwell

Streeten, Paul, and Thomas Balogh (1957) 'A Reconsideration of Monetary Policy', *Bulletin of the Oxford University Institute of Statistics*, **19**: 331–9

Sylos-Labini, Paolo (1984) *The Forces of Economic Growth and Decline*, Cambridge, Ma: MIT Press

Tanzi, Vito (1977) 'Inflation, Lags in Collection, and the Real Value of Tax Revenue', *International Monetary Fund Staff Papers*, **24**: 154–67

Taylor, Lance (1983) *Structuralist Macroeconomics*, New York: Basic Books

——(1987a) 'Economic Openness: Problems to Century's End', Helsinki: WIDER

——(1987b) *Stabilization and Growth in Developing Countries: A Structuralist Approach*, New York: Harwood Academic Publishers

——(1987c) 'IMF Conditionality: Incomplete Theory, Policy Malpractice', in Robert J. Myers (ed.) *The Political Morality of the International Monetary Fund*, New Brunswick, NJ: Transaction Books

——, Kadir T. Yurukoglu, and Shahid A. Chaudhry (1986) 'A Macro Model of an Oil Exporter—Nigeria', in J. Peter Neary and Sweder van Wijnbergen (eds.) *Natural Resources and the Macroeconomy*, Oxford: Basil Blackwell

Toye, John (1987) 'Varieties of Stabilization Experience: A Comment', Brighton: Institute of Development Studies, University of Sussex

Tseng, Wanda (1984) 'The Effects of Adjustment', *Finance and Development*, **21** (no. 4): 2–5

van der Hoeven, Rolph, and Jan Vandemoortele (1986) 'Kenya: Stabilization and Adjustment Experiences (1979–85) and Prospects for Future Development', Helsinki: WIDER

van Wijnbergen, Sweder (1983) 'Credit Policy, Inflation, and Growth in a Financially Repressed Economy', *Journal of Development Economics*, **13**: 45–65

Vilas, Carlos (1984) 'Unidad Nacional y Contradicciones Sociales en una Economia Mixta: Nicaragua 1979–84' in R. Harris and C. Vilas (eds.) *La Revolucion en Nicaragua*, Mexico City: Ediciones Era

Webb, Richard (1987) 'Stabilization Policy: Peru 1980–85', Helsinki: WIDER

INDEX

absorption 20, 36, 126, 153, 160
  and exports 30, 36–7, 153
accelerator 30, 100
Allende, Salvador 32, 117
appreciation (of exchange rate) 9, 19,
  45, 76, 102, 103
Argentina 3, 12, 13, 14-15, 16, 17, 20,
  21, 22, 32, 34, 36, 37, 46, 49, 51,
  60, 61–2, 65–6, 121–4, 142–5, 154,
  168
assets 35
austerity 8, 12, 19–20, 27, 43, 48, 51,
  63–4, 83–4, 114, 117, 121, 126,
  142–3

bail-out (financial) 37, 53, 65–6, 95,
  112, 120, 122, 125, 140, 153
Bolivia 64 n.
bonanza, foreign 18–20, 35, 94–109
Brazil 3, 11, 15, 17, 21, 32, 36, 37, 41,
  46, 47, 48, 50, 51, 60, 61–2,
  124–9, 142–5, 168

capacity utilization 11
capital flight 14, 19, 22, 48, 51–2, 65,
  100, 122, 153
capital inflow 14, 48, 51, 65, 86, 89,
  103–4, 107, 112, 114, 121–2, 139,
  153–4
capital market 14, 52, 99
causality (in models) 12, 19, 38
Chicago boys 119 n.
Chile 3, 13 n., 14, 17, 35, 51, 64,
  117–21, 142–5
Chun Doo Whan 141
class 13, 20–3
closure (of models) 5, 19, 26, 38, 56
Colombia 3, 18–19, 34, 35, 44, 48, 50,
  51, 52, 66, 94–9, 142–5, 150, 153
conditionality 2, 154–9
contra (Nicaragua) 79–80
crawling peg 14, 42, 44, 49, 65, 95,
  125, 152
  active 14, 64 n., 122
  passive 64 n., 152
credit limits 156–7

creditors 13

debtors 13, 22–3
demand creation 15
depreciation, *see* devaluation
devaluation (of exchange rate) 9, 22,
  35–6, 47, 48–9, 62, 86, 88, 112,
  114, 119, 121, 125, 135, 140
  contradictory 42–3, 100, 151
  expansionary 43–4
  real 35, 99
disasters 16, 37–8, 130–2
Dutch disease 19 n., 35

Egypt 3, 19, 21, 33, 35, 36, 46, 52, 66,
  67 n., 107–9, 142–5
Engel's law 34
equation of exchange 10, 12, 39, 58,
  155
excess demand 10
exchange controls 13, 15, 18, 48, 52–3,
  95, 99–100, 152
exchange rate 9
  multiple 66–7, 107, 117
  overvalued 15, 48–9, 119, 152
  real 35
export subsidies 50, 112, 139, 153
exports 17, 30, 36, 42, 102, 107, 112,
  130, 139
  manufactured 36
  primary 17
  response to output level 30, 36–7
external debt 15, 36, 54, 103, 113,
  120, 125, 139–40
external strangulation 18, 37, 40,
  76–94

financial
  crisis 13–14, 51, 60, 95, 112, 119–20
  depression (deepening) 56 n., 139 n.
  fragility 64–6, 122, 153
  instruments 52
  intermediation 56–7
  programming 5, 150, 154–9
  regulation 13–14, 57

ponondrum